Chapter 1: Conspiracy Theory Defined

"The very word mystery is offensive in a free and open society; and we as a group innately and generally went against to secret social orders, to secret pledges and to secret proceedings."

~ John F. Kennedy, April 27th 1961,

Definition of Conspiracy Theory

The expression, "fear inspired notion," is characterized by Ben Goertzel as "a clarification for an occasion or circumstance that summons a connivance by evil and strong gatherings, regularly political in inspiration." According to the Merriam-Webster word reference, "the meaning of paranoid notion is a hypothesis that clarifies an occasion or situation as the consequence of a mystery plot by normally strong plotters" (Goertzel, 1994; Merriam-Webster, n.d.).

Different Types of Conspiracy Theories

Once you start investigating paranoid notions, it resembles getting the finish of a monstrous bundle of yarn that requests disentangling. It's winding up in a labyrinth where each corner uncovers another piece of information to addressing another riddle or tracking down your direction through to the opposite side. This has been my involvement with revealing and finding explicit confirmation to help different paranoid ideas. These theories are appearing on message boards on the dark web and social media channels such as Facebook, Twitter, Instagram, YouTube, and even on Pinterest.

Despite these web-based media associations attempting to get rid of scheme fan, something really doesn't add up about QAnon that is unique in relation to the rest. As fast as one page or site is shut down, another springs up elsewhere. Whoever Q is, they are absolutely no moron, and know precisely how to manage innovation to receive their message out. Moreover, they're not addressing inquiries concerning what's happening to such an extent as they are raising new questions.

They pass on enigmatic signs to where answers might be found and lead the people who need to know reality to all the ideal places.

Those that have read up fear inspired notions for quite a long time have arranged them into various gatherings as demonstrated underneath. By researching each unique paranoid fear you can choose for yourself where every one of the central participants brought should squeeze into these definitions. Michael Barkun, teacher emeritus of political theory at Syracuse University, while work in political radicalism and the connection among religion and savagery, has done broad exploration on paranoid notions also. His arrangement of paranoid notions into the accompanying three sorts has been broadly used by other people who do top to bottom investigations of scheme theories.

Barkun's Three Types

1. Event-based fear inspired notions like 9/11, the Kennedy death, the spread of AIDS, and, surprisingly, the Coronavirus Pandemic has been included along with the remaining blend of this kind of trick theory.
2. Next is fundamental based fear inspired notions which depend on single gatherings or people who are hellbent on penetrating networks to acquire control. The vast majority of these are done in

a cryptic way with numerous ceremonies occurring away from public scrutiny. Numerous speculations of this sort are related with gatherings like Freemasons, Communism, or the Catholic Church. Others in an alternate vein, yet additionally subjects of foundational based paranoid ideas, incorporate the Bilderberg Group and the Illuminati.

3. The third is delegated super fear inspired notions where various paranoid notions are finely interlaced with each other (Barkun, 2oo3).

Shallow Versus Deep

Murray Rothbard, a political scholar and monetary antiquarian, placed that there were two explicit kinds of paranoid fears, the first being "shallow" and the other being "profound." The distinction between the two could be recognized basically as per Rothbard. In the main case, the inquiry that one could pose is "who stands to profit from this?" and the second, profound fear inspired notions are those where you explicitly need to proceed to burrow to observe the responses you're searching for (Rothbard, 2006).

Walker's Five

Jesse Walker, book manager for Reason Magazine, has had articles in various editorial distributions, generally with a freedom supporter inclining. Nonetheless, his 2013 book entitled The United States of Paranoia*: A Conspiracy Theory distinguishes five arrangements of paranoid fears that*, not at all like Barkun's three sorts which classify the " type" of paranoid fear, depend on the style and direction that the hypotheses take.

1. "Foes outside" speculations allude to people or gatherings that are compromising networks or conditions from the outside.
2. "Adversaries inside" relates to schemers that are straightforwardly essential for the general public in which you are living. You might be living nearby to them, working with them, or even involved with them and you will never at any point suspect their involvement.
3. "Foes above" allude to people who stand firm on strong footings who can change the plan to suit their own means, controlling

others in the process.

4. "Adversaries underneath" are an incredible inverse of the above hypothesis. This would incorporate the essential common who are ready to rebel against the "foundation" to compel change.
5. "Kind connivances" are other-worldly or gallant people or gatherings who work unobtrusively in the background to make the world a superior spot to live (Walker, 2014).

How Conspiracy Theory Influences Individuals

Conspiracy speculations can impact people or gatherings in different ways. For

the most part they can't continuously be demonstrated which is the reaAlong these linesn they are alluded to as a hypothesis. It ought to be noted, notwithstanding, that a case that something is only a paranoid fear and ought to be dismissed as guiltless or outlandish doesn't really work everything out. Hypotheses that are excused are regularly the absolute most intricate and perilous paranoid ideas of all. These might appear up to this point brought with the end goal that it's basically impossible that that you should be approving what the gossip factory is talking about. So, how could such an enormous gathering concoct a similar story on numerous occasions (Cherry, 2019)?

According to history specialist Kathryn S. Olmsted, there are a few justifications for why Americans are so inclined to succumbing to fear inspired notions; models incorporate the following:

- Secrecy inside the public authority in regards to explicit activities later became exposed, for example, Watergate, Project MK-Ultra and the CIA's arrangement with the crowd to kill the head of Cuba, Fidel Castro.
- Sanctioned government conspiracy theories and propaganda present such as the claim that Saddam Hussein was responsible for the 9/11 attacks on the Twin Towers and the World Trade Center. Other exposed hypotheses incorporate the attack of the USA by Germany during World War II.
- The public authority's ceaselessly utilizes shrewd strategies with regards to keeping an eye on those they accept ought not be relied upon

(Olmstead, 2019)

The New World Order

The New World Order (NWO) paranoid notion comeS from the picture on the rear of the American seal. This conveys the Latin message of “novus ordo seclorum” which means “New Order of the Ages.” This picture has been on the opposite side of the American seal beginning around 1782 and has showed up on the rear of the U.S. one-dollar note beginning around 1935 (The Great Seal of the United States, n.d.).

While Scheme scholars guarantee the image on the rear of the U.S. one-dollar note with the pyramid and the divine eye addresses the secret society known as the Illuminati, this might be more convoluted. With the flow pandemic spinning out of control across the globe, I’m alluding to COVID-19 that is overturning economies, and affecting the texture of each general public all through the world.

Some could accept this was a man-made illness, however there are excesses of moving parts for this to be so. The inquiry top of the personalities of the greater part of the world’s contracting populace concerns what the world will resemble post COVID-19. I think a great many people concur that we will always avoid the manner in which life was preceding this pandemic. Some connivance scholars keep on accepting that this is a man-made infection for monetary profiteering.

One normal case among these scholars is that Dr. Anthony Fauci, head of the National Institute of Allergy and Infectious Diseases and Bill Gates are the geniuses behind this pandemic. Their principle purpose for the pandemic is to hold onto power and benefit monetarily through vaccinations.

For all this talk of a New World Order coming into power, if one really analyzes the aftermath of death and destruction across the globe right now, thanks to the global pandemic, it’s more likely that this New World Order will never be realized.

The Deep State

There’s a great deal of information as of now concerning whether the

"Underground government" is a fear inspired notion or regardless of whether it's an authentic danger to the American government. Here's creator of In Deep*: The FBI, the CIA, and the Truth About America's "Secret government"*, David Rhode's interpretation of the circumstance: while numerous Americans essentially excuse the hypothesis that there are dull powers working inside the public authority, set on pointing fingers at Trump, Rhode accepts that POTUS has an issue on his hands. He asserts that the "secret government is both a genuine article and a poisonous interruption". A top to bottom meeting with Sean Illing from Vox, New Yorker manager and creator, affirms the justification for why Trump deferred responding to the underlying Covid pandemic was because of fears and worries about the "covert government" inside his own government.

Here's what Rhode affirms in this interview:

> *"The secret government isn't by and large an apparition. There are portions of the US government that employ genuine power outside the traditional governing rules of the framework. It's anything but an intrigue against Trump, however the term alludes to something that does exist."*

He alludes to government organizations such as the CIA, FBI and NSA that have the potential to monitor everybody, thanks to advancements in technology. These associations represent a danger to the American public and their privileges to security and straightforwardness from the public authority. Not Trump has control enough over these associations any longer, that is assuming he could possibly do in any case. As we go further into these examinations you will see that there will be more organizations and people in key situations inside these offices going crazy and it's all for the sake of first change privileges and opportunity of speech.

David affirms that these offices need "a forceful oversight." Rhode lets Illings know that one of the fundamental purposes behind composing his book was that a 2018 study found that around 70% of US residents accept there's a mystery gathering of people who are controlling all that occurs in Washington. A further 80 percent are persuaded they are under reconnaissance by the public authority. The greater part of those accepting this are supportive of right wing.

Additional remarks made by Rhode in this equivalent meeting state that assuming there are government employees despondent working for the Trump Administration, they ought to simply stop rather than attempting to assume control over issues. There have been the right governing rules set up to guarantee that majority rules government is fit as a fiddle in the United States in light of their discretionary framework. Permitting other government authorities to go around and do whatever they might feel like doing can turn out to be very hazardous for sure (Illing, 2020).

The Swamp

"Emptying out the wasteland" is a term that has been tossed around the United States Government since the 1800's the place where it was first utilized by Helen Hunt Jackson. Washington DC was accepted to be based on swampland, such a great deal the first wording and references were focused on in a real sense Draining the swampland to control mosquitos and jungle fever episodes. Agreeing to

Rebecca Harrington, in her piece named "This is what Trump implies when he says, 'Empty out the badland' - despite the fact that it's anything but an exact analogy." *As found in Business Insider in 2016*. (Harrington, 2016).

According to the Political Dictionary: "Clean out the badland is a similitude that means to uncover defilement. It's not unexpected utilized in governmental issues. Donald Trump didn't coin [the phrase]." On October eighteenth, 2016, Trump tweeted, *"I will Make Our Government Honest Again - trust me. Above all, I will have to #DrainTheSwamp in DC."*

The Awakening Defined

Awakenings are alluded to since the beginning of time as places where there have been strict recoveries and individuals have "woken" up to various realities. Every restoration has filled a need and come about in various "developments" starting. This extraordinary arousing will be different in that it's to be the last incredible arousing. This enlivening is talked about in predictions of old where great and insidious will at long last wage war for the spirits of all humankind for one final time. Sounding excessively scriptural and fantastical? It has forever been composed that Satan will walk the earth having ability to ruin the hearts and psyches of humankind until the last fight begins.

This will be the last incredible fight where Satan and his flunkies get to fight straightforwardly with Jesus Christ and his adherents. For any scriptural researchers out there, the finish of times has effectively been composed and the outcomes are known, in any case, this doesn't imply that the underlying fight won't happen. How prepared would you say you are for this confrontation? The battlefronts are being laid out right as we speak.

Dark powers of evil have been permitted to work on the earth for a really long time. Individuals submitting disasters so intolerable and unreasonable might be your neighbors, they might sit close to you in chapel on a Sunday, they might be the one pressing your food, leaving your vehicle, you might be working for them or they might even be governing you in the upper echelons of power right now! These dark forces are erecting buildings and demonic temples that have statues of Baphomet which has the head of a goat and according to Time Magazine, "after hundreds of years… is presently the emblem of contemporary Satanism"

(Jenkins, 2015).

This huge figure that gauges two or three tons wears what looks like a strict corona behind the top of the goat, with a Satanic pentagram cut inside it. This sculpture has some notable evil images cut in and around it, as well as two little youngsters on one or the other side, gazing up at the sculpture like hypnotized by Baphomet. It's all around reported and perceived just like the image for The Satanic Temple and their devotees. Assuming that the participation at the divulging of this sculpture was anything to go by, there were more than 700 individuals. They can't be generally curious to see what was genuinely going on with the fight. Obviously Satanism is without a doubt alive and very well in the United States. Ian Richardson, a journalist for USA Today, exposes claims via online media that this or these sculptures exist in general visibility. He proceeds to say that as per the Church of Satan's site, there is just a single sculpture which is on private property and away from prying eyes.

The Church of Satan was officially settled in 2013 as a not-for-benefit strict association. They additionally decry the first church that was established by Anton Le Vey in 1966. It has been affirmed by Co-organizer of this strict request, Malcom Jarry, that the real sculpture is inside on private property in Salem (Richardson, 2020).

Baphomet

Where does the name Baphomet come from? Here begins one more piece of the riddle that integrates all of this going back millennia to 1100 AD where a considerable lot of the Templar Knights admitted to venerating the icon, Baphomet.

The current sculpture of Baphomet depends on the picture drawn by Eliphas Levi, a French medium in 1856. It first showed up in quite a while book, *Transcendental Magic: It's Doctrine and Ritual.* A comparable picture as the current sculpture shows Baphomet as a winged bisexual with a pentagram on his temple, a light between his horns and wings. The two-fingered salute addresses the old compositions on the emerald tablet taken from Hermes Trismegistus which states "As above, so below."

On each arm the Latin words SOLVE, importance to isolate, and COAGULA, to join are apparent. This alludes to the ideas of restricting and slackening. While the first drawing by Levi showed a transsexual being, the current Church of Satan concluded that they weren't going to outrage anybody by attempting to be socially sensitive thus decided to select the youngster and the young man in the new portrayal all things being equal. There is as yet a Caduceus on the chest of the sculpture; the imagery here's intriguing for the rest of this book. "It represents exchange, dealings, and correspondence," as indicated by James Morgan from BBC News (Morgan, 2015).

The main focal point from this section is that the New World Order, The Deep State and The Great Awakening are for the most part genuine, however that there are paranoid notions that are simply guessed and made to appear to be genuine by their relationship with these concepts.

Chapter 2: Theories Throughout History

"Everything is a connivance. Individuals In this wayrt of belittle the word. But a conspiracy is when two people get together and do something. So, assuming more than one individual accomplishes something, it's a trick. The insurgency was a trick, Iran, Contra, Watergate."

~ Richard Belzer

Assassinations to Actresses

If there have been murders and disorder made by "the foundation" for the sake of "everyone's benefit," these will constantly be wrapped with mystery and people will yell, "paranoid notion." With TV presented in 1935, correspondence and innovation would become interwoven. It would turn out to be more challenging for state run administrations, worldwide pioneers, and those looking for the New World Order (NWO) to be quieted. It would likewise break any miniscule piece of proof into many various pieces to permit the populace to arrive at their own conclusions.

With the send off of the web during the 1980s, there would be no preventing any connivance devotee from hooking onto recent developments, posing awkward inquiries that those in the most elevated workplaces in state run administrations, governments, and tyrannies would have rather not reply. Large numbers of these inquiries would go back millennia. With the end goal of curtness and space in this book, we are simply going to think back similarly as Abraham Lincoln and spotlight predominantly on the United States.

President Abraham Lincoln

Imagine yourself in 1865, it's a warm evening in Washington D.C. furthermore the American Civil War has recently reached a conclusion. President Robert E. Lee, the Confederate General, gave up himself and his huge armed force on April ninth in

Virginia. President Abraham Lincoln and his significant other, Mary Todd Lincoln, showed up at the Ford Theater. They involve a corner straight over the stage with Henry Rathbone, and Clara Harris, his fiancée.

John Wilkes Booth had devised a course of action to hijack the President to impact the Civil War for the Confederates. Whenever General Lee gave up, this threw Booth's arrangement off course. Hearing that the President would be at the theater that evening, the capturing plot transformed into something way more evil. At precisely 10:15 pm, John Wilkes Booth slipped into the container, pointed a .44-type derringer gun to the President's head, and discharged. Whenever Rathbone hurried to assault him, Booth hopped onto the stage and yelled the Virginia State Motto, "Sic semper tyrannis!" ("Thus, ever to tyrants!")

The President got consideration quickly from a clinical specialist who had been in the crowd. A few troopers moved the President to a motel across the road from the theater. At the point when the top health spokesperson showed up, he demonstrated it was suspicious he would last the evening. At 7:22 am the next morning, April 15, 1865, the President was at long last articulated dead. He was just 56 years of age at the time.

What isn't so well been aware of this death is that it was a plot to overturn the whole American government at that point and not simply kill Lincoln. Before Lee gave up, Ulysses S. Award, William Seaward, and the Vice-President, Andrew Johnson were completely expected to be together in one spot. This was really an arranged rebellion that had fizzled. While Booth assaulted Lincoln, the arranged assault on the Vice President self-destructed and Seaward endure the assault on himself (History.com Editors, 2018).

From the second President Lincoln passed on, there was far and wide hypothesis that in spite of the fact that Booth had discharged the deadly shot, he was certainly not the driving force behind the death. The public found it difficult to accept that a simple entertainer might have coordinated three extra way endeavored deaths of Grant, Seaward and Johnson. Papers on the morning of the President's demise printed bogus data and bits of gossip started to take the country far and wide. Albeit Seaward made due, in specific distributions it was accounted for that he had passed on alongside the President. Some were persuaded that the Confederates had entirely won.

The President of the Confederates, Jefferson Davies was under the magnifying instrument for some time. It was trusted that Judah P. Benjamin, a revolutionary, Jewish Secretary of State for the Confederates was sufficiently naughty to have completed such a plan. Benjamin was a suspect for two reasons, first and foremost on the grounds that he was Jewish, and besides in light of the fact that he had close associations with the Rothschild family (the rich investors). The motivation behind why the Rothschilds could have needed Lincoln dead was a direct result of his financial strategy. Hostile to Semetic suggestions were additionally indicated in light of the fact that Benjamin was Jewish and the Rothschilds were Jewish. As per scheme scholars, "that was exactly what the Jews did."

Others accused the Catholics and it was even inferred that the Pope himself was some way or another elaborate when enemies of outsiders, hostile to semetic, against catholic activists turned out to be important for this paranoid fear. This hypothesis seethed on for a really long time and has been returned to exactly 129 years following his assasination. Who were the central parts behind the Lincoln death? Given the way that General Lee had as of now given up himself and the Civil War was finished. Who might have taken over from him? Had Lincoln made due, what might America resemble today? We won't ever have the responses to these inquiries, they kicked the bucket close by Lincoln and Booth (Goldfield, 2019).

The Kennedy's

President John F. Kennedy

The first of the Kennedy's to be killed was President John F. Kennedy in Dallas Texas while driving in a motorcade on November 22nd, 1963. His death was credited to Lee Harvey Oswald who was captured right away a short time later. Thus lies perhaps the biggest trick throughout the entire existence of the United States, or potentially even the world. Not long after being captured, Lee Harvey Oswald was shot dead by Jack Ruby. Questions stay with respect to who else was engaged with this connivance and plot to kill the President. Fingers point towards the CIA, FBI and even the KGB, who all confirm that Oswald worked alone. It was excessively convoluted for Oswald to only be a disappointed sharp-shooting ex-marine. Oswald had deserted to the Soviet Union in 1959. Denied super durable home he got back to the States. In 1963 he once again

applied to the USSR to venture out to Cuba. This solicitation is again denied.

Apparently this 24-year-old acted totally alone. He was anarchistic and against the framework that President Kennedy represented. Oswald denied any association with the shooting, guaranteeing he was only the "patsy"! Helpfully for whoever set him up, no one will at any point know who the genuine players were (J.Harrington and Wood, 2020; Brown, 2017; Smith, 2013).

The Warren Commission

The Warren Commission set up by President Lyndon B. Johnson finished a full examination concerning the death of President Kennedy. The discoveries of this commission reasoned that Oswald followed up on his own. Sadly, in spite of their earnest attempts, the trick factory keeps on turning with respect to this death. Jack Ruby who killed Oswald likewise helpfully passes on in a matter of seconds before his preliminary starts in 1967. Albeit 30,000 unredacted records have been delivered encompassing this death there are more due for discharge in October 2021. In spite of their earnest attempts, this is one of those connivances that actually will not disappear! (Public

Archives and The Warren Commission, 2018).

Senator Robert Kennedy

Only two months after the demise of Martin Luther King Jr. broken the country, another critical death happens at the Ambassador inn in Los Angeles. In the early hours of the morning, Senator Robert Kennedy was well on his way towards winning the decisions. This might have prompted one more Kennedy in the White House. Not long after modeling for certain photographic artists, a few shots were discharged. Bobby Kennedy promptly droops to the floor. Those standing nearest to the alleged shooter, a 24-year-old Jordanian evacuee, Sirhan, distinguish him as the culprit. He had composed that "Kennedy should be killed before June 5, 1968." His thinking behind this "declaration" was that it was "the principal commemoration of the Six Day War between Israel, Egypt, Syria, and Jordan." According to the Los Angeles Times, Kennedy kicked the bucket at 1:44 am on the morning of June sixth, 1968 (J. Harrington and Wood, 2020).

Having taken in their example with Oswald, Sirhan was very much secured so minimal possibility of him was being killed prior to going to preliminary. Around fifty years after the fact, Robert Kennedy Jr. visited Sirhan in jail, leaving with a larger number of inquiries than responds to. As indicated by Sirhan, he was not by any means the only shooter. This was the kind of thing that had been suspected for quite a while. One more strange homicide and the feared revile against the Kennedy family was starting to unfurl. Today, the Ambassador Hotel is no more. It was crushed to clear a path for schools that were required nearby. On one of the dividers is an image of Robert Kennedy with the renowned words conveyed in a discourse in South Africa two years before his passing: "Scarcely any will have the significance to twist history; however every one of us can attempt to change a little part of the occasions, and altogether, these demonstrations will be written throughout the entire existence of this age" (Shalby, 2018).

Kennedy was just 42 at that point. Winning California during that year's essential political race was a major advance towards emulating his sibling John's example. America had been in disturbance since the mid 1960s when his sibling was killed. With Robert's demise happening so near that of Dr. Martin Luther King Jr. questions were being inquired. Had Bobby Kennedy came to the White House, the Vietnamese conflict might have appeared to be very unique for Americans. With the second Kennedy death, questions and trick scholars started puzzling over whether the whole family was some way or another cursed.

While a considerable lot of the reports have been delivered in regards to the death of John F. Kennedy have been delivered for the world to acquire more noteworthy bits of knowledge, large numbers of these archives were set apart as "insignificant." Most scholars actually have many inquiries in regards to one of the most popular occasions of the century. There is still a lot of uncertainty encompassing whether Lee Harvey Oswald and Jack Ruby acted alone. Whenever examinations were resumed in 1976 it was concurred that there was likely a second shooter on "the green meadow." The slope gave a greatly improved vantage point for the shooter.

Further inquiries were raised concerning "a man conveying an umbrella." Louie Steven Witt was gotten on film raising this umbrella out of sight at the specific time that the shots rang out. Regardless of whether this was a sign for another person, or him shooting a toxic substance dart. This was exposed during a meeting with Witt in 1978 who admitted that he was uniquely there to "irritate the president."

Was it a crowd hit? Coming about because of the plans that Kennedy had for Fidel Castro at that point. Jimmy Hoffa and the teamsters were as a rule firmly researched by Robert Kennedy in his situation as Secretary of State. Would all the shaking of enclosures among Castro and Hoffa be able to irritate the crowd adequately that all of this wound up misfiring on the Kennedy siblings. Bobby Kenedy was persuaded that if anybody somehow managed to be killed, it would be him and not his sibling John.

One of different hypotheses was that it was a CIA hit. There were bits of hearsay that a part of the CIA had split away and they were liable for Kennedy's death (Halleman, 2017).

Senator Edward Kennedy

1969 saw Senator Edward Kennedy in a genuine mishap in Massachusetts where a young lady going with him was lethally harmed. Questions emerge regarding whether he was intended to bite the dust in this equivalent mishap. Once again, were darker forces at play on this fateful night? Who was the young woman travelling with him? Was this possibly another Kennedy hit that had gone awfully wrong (J. Harrington and Wood, 2020)?

John F. Kennedy Jr.

The child of the late President, John F. Kennedy Jr. was killed in a plane accident on July 16, 1999 close to Martha's Vineyard. He was flying with his better half, Carolyn Bessette Kennedy and her sister Lauren Bessette. The single propeller plane collided with the Atlantic Ocean and the debacle is accused on "spatial confusion." Data from radar affirms that the plane dropped around 1,100 feet in fourteen seconds. Notwithstanding a broad quest for survivors, following a few days it goes to a surveillance mission to track down the destruction. This was at long last found by Navy jumpers on July 21, 1999. The plane was submerged 8 miles off the shoreline of Martha's Vineyard. The scourge of the Kennedy's proceeds with today with individuals from the family kicking the bucket strangely like clockwork (Editors, 2020).

Religious Leaders

Malcolm X

Malcolm X was killed in 1965 by three revolutionary individuals from Islam. In spite of the fact that he was regularly connected with Martin Luther King Jr., their messages were incomprehensibly unique. While Martin Luther King Jr. was about harmony and equity, Malcolm X trusted in revolutionary change regardless of whether this implied inducing brutality to convey the idea. His extreme convictions were regularly an interesting issue with the Nation of Islam causing a split. It's accepted this split was liable for the Nation of Islam requesting he be killed. It hadn't been a year since he had cut attaches with the gathering and which of the shooters had really killed him is as yet a secret today (J. Harrington and Wood, 2020).

Although three men were arrested, Talmage Hayer and two others, it's likely that the second two shooters were incorrectly implicated in the shooting. The gathering liable for his shooting, the Nation of Islam (NOI) had really given Malcolm X his name. He had been one of their most passionate advocates of religion for over 10 years, ascending through their positions. Offering an inappropriate remark following the death of President John F. Kennedy in December 1963, the head of the NOI development, Muhammad prohibited Malcolm X for a time of ninety days. This goaded him and before the finish of this multi day time span, he broke attaches with the NOI.

What was much more dreadful was that Malcolm X made an association that was contrary to the NOI. Since he stood firm on a very conspicuous foothold inside the NOI he knew a great deal regarding the inward operations. He knew such a large number of hazardous things regarding Muhammad's own life and mystery infidileties. This might actually undermine the NOI. Regardless of whether this was the justification for his death won't ever be known. Could he have utilized the data that he needed to ruin their association? Conceivably, given the idea of who Malcolm X was. Was the perfect man considered responsible for his death? Intrigue scholars have long accepted that this isn't true and following fifty years, this death as well as that of Martin Luther King Jr. are being reopened.

Dr. Martin Luther King Jr.

Martin Luther King Jr. was killed on April fourth, 1968. Ruler had been visiting Tennessee to talk at a congregation rally in Memphis on April third. On the

evening of the fourth, en route to a supper with a Memphis serve, he ventures onto the overhang of his lodging. A solitary shot is discharged, smacking him in the face. Albeit hurried to a close by medical clinic, he was articulated dead at 7:05 pm. In excess of 100,000 grievers followed the burial service parade. Soon after his death, a rifle and ammo were seen as close to the lodging that King was remaining in. Fingerprints had a place with got away from convict James Earl Ray.

Meanwhile, Ray figured out how to escape the country to Britain. A global manhunt prompts Ray's capture on July nineteenth, 1968. To get away from capital punishment, he concedes to the homicide. In this lies the fear inspired notion. Not long after he is condemned to a 99-year jail term, Ray abjures his admission. Many inquiries have been posed to whether he worked alone or regardless of whether he was working thick as thieves with the CIA or Ku Klux Klan (KKK). Beam kept on announcing his honesty, guaranteeing he was set up by somebody known as "Raoul." His attorney figured out how to get the case returned and gotten help from the King family that he had been improperly denounced. One more individual near being justified for improper imprisonment kicked the bucket in jail in 1998 (J. Harrington and Wood, 2020).

Actresses

Marilyn Monroe

Did Marilyn Monroe truly end it all? This is another paranoid fear that in all likelihood will not disappear. Following guessed illegal undertakings with both the President, John F. Kennedy and Robert Kennedy, Secretary General at that point, it's accepted the last call Marilyn made was to the White House. A few things don't make any sense in regards to her unexpected passing and being tracked down exposed on her bed in the early long stretches of August 4, 1962. There were speculations she'd been experiencing psychological instability and breakdowns for some time. These brought about her being terminated from a few films. Notwithstanding, at the hour of her demise, it's accepted that she showed up very energetic and positive without precedent for quite a while. The day preceding her passing, she had marked new agreements for extra motion pictures. She was certain with regards to the home she'd just

purchased and wanted to remodel it herself. Following a discussion she had with her specialist, he had voiced concerns and mentioned that her own servant stay with her that evening.

According to the individuals who knew her best, she had a background marked by sorrow and substance misuse. It was typical for her to need to quit shooting a film to be conceded to medical clinic to detox for her to finish a film. She was crushed when her union with eminent dramatist Arthur Miller reached a conclusion in 1961.

The day she passed on, Marilyn met with a few people. She was marking contracts for impending film bargains which would occur before very long. She talked with Peter Lawford, an individual entertainer. This was accepted to have been her last discussion with anybody. Becoming restless after a portion of the things she told Lawford on the telephone, he took a stab at calling her therapist with no profit. At last, he got hold of her attorney who called the house and talked with Marilyn's own servant who guaranteed him that everything was fine.

Eunice, Marilyn's servant, got up at around 3.30 am on August 5, 1963 incapable to get into the room since it had been locked from within. Now she calls Dr. Greenson, Marilyn's therapist who encourages her to go outside to see whether she could see anything through the window. Eunice does as such, finding the celebrity lying exposed face down on her bed, telephone grasped in one hand and a note with a phone number for the White House in the other (Lavender, 2020).

Here comes the connivance Marilyn had talked about ending it all before with one of her kindred entertainers. She'd expressed that assuming she were to at any point make it happen, she would dress in a white robe, have both her hair and cosmetics done, take an excess of dozing tablets and hit the sack. Here is the difference:

Marilyn was found on her bed, stripped. She was face down and not lying calmly like she'd said she would be. Her hair was screwed up and she wasn't wearing any cosmetics. There were different medications viewed as close to her on her end table. Nonetheless, These medications were different to what in particular was found in her framework during her examination. Undeniable degrees of chloral hydrate (a narcotic to treat a sleeping disorder utilized before clinical tasks) found in her circulation system. These were excused in light of the fact that she had ingested every one of the dozing tablets inside a short space of time. Despite the fact that Marilyn was known to have a liquor and substance misuse issue, she was notable to blend her beverages (champagne and vodka) and afterward pop pills each in turn. This was her example of managing things. The coroner composed on her passing testament that it was a "potential self destruction," however the press and public weren't accepting it.

Close companions of Marilyn's were yelling "coverup" on the premise that she had such a large number of plans arranged for the next few days. Those nearest to her asserted that she was more joyful than she'd been in quite a while. She was apparently chipping away at getting back with ex, Joe

DiMaggio.

Many years after the fact, a coroner affirmed that he had to sign that she'd passed on from a lethal excess in spite of absence of proof of the medication that killed her anyplace in her room. Questions were raised why her house keeper was washing her bed material in the early hours of the morning while the police were attempting to explore the scene. Joe DiMaggio paid all her burial service expenses and set up for red roses to be set at her grave three times each week for the following twenty years.

Although the case was returned in 1982, there was not a lot to continue separated from more inquiries and a secretive injury found on her body. Most data highlighted treachery yet by who? The Kennedy's were at first accused as a result of her inclusion with both JFK and Robert Kennedy. It was said that they did it to safeguard the picture of JFK. Similarly as there are as yet numerous unanswered inquiries concerning the Kennedy deaths, no one truly realizes what occurred with Norma Jean Mortenson, otherwise called Marilyn Monroe on that portentous evening (Dimuro, 2019; J. Harrington and Wood, 2020; Louise, 2020).

Natalie Wood

Four individuals moved on board the yacht, Splendor, on November 28, 1981- notable Hollywood entertainer, Natalie Wood, her significant other, Robert Wagner, individual entertainer Christopher Walken, and the commander of the yacht, Dennis Davern. The couple were known for taking their yacht to

Catalina Island. Having partaken in a feast at an eatery on Catalina Island, the proprietor of the café was concerned whether they would effectively make it back to the Splendor by means of their dinghy. He was worried to such an extent that he called Kurt Craig from harbor watch to verify they showed up securely. The four had left the eatery at 10:30 pm.

Once on board the Splendor, Wagner and Walken got into a warmed contention over something. Different travelers report that around 11:05 the notification that both the dinghy and Natalie Wood are no place to be found.

It's just at 1:30 am that the primary "transport to-shore" call is made and a further two hours after this at 3:30 am that the coast watch is reached. What the vast majority see as intriguing and detract from the vanishing of Natalie Wood is the four-hour time delay. Her body was found at around 8 am just a pretty far from their yacht at a secluded inlet at the Blue Cavern Point.

On November 30, 1981, the clinical analyst played out a post-mortem takes note of her blood liquor level and chalked every one of the injuries all around her face, arms and legs to be reliable with a fall as she was attempting to move on board the dinghy. The clinical analyst leads her passing an accident.

September 1, 1997, Christopher Walken adds to what exactly happened that evening by let The Hollywood Reporter know that it had been coming down that evening and portions of the yacht were exceptionally tricky. He affirms that she had hit the sack before them and the dinghy was making a clamor against the side of the yacht. One more snippet of data given by him is that she was unable to swim. He affirms that she had a coat on and had most likely gone to move the dinghy so it would quit making a clamor against the boat, refering to there was an incline that was incredibly elusive. The remainder of his meeting becomes obscure where he discusses passing and not having any desire to bite the dust.

November 17, 2011-the case encompassing the demise of Natalie Wood is abruptly returned. New proof and data are submitted to the police through mysterious sources. The next day, the skipper of the yacht, Davern lets the police know that he had lied at the hour of her demise and he

embroils Wagner.

By January 14, 2013, her reason for death was changed from "unplanned suffocating" to "suffocating and other unsure elements." What the clinical inspector had not had the option to demonstrate at the hour of her passing was actually how and when the injuries all around her body were supported. On February 1, 2018 Robert Wagner was at last named as an individual of interest in the demise of his better half. At the point when stood up to on camera by their little girl in 2020, Robert Wagner denies having a say in his significant other's passing and their little girl affirms that she trusts him. The secret remaining parts strange today (Bilyeau, 2018; Roberts, 2020).

Conspiracy hypotheses have existed nearly since long before recorded history. What is separating this hypothesis from all others. We will think about different speculations and what has or is energizing them in the parts that follow (Finstad, 2020).

Chapter 3: Conspiracy Theory 2020

"When you're youthful, you check TV and think, there's a scheme out. The organizations have contrived to imbecilic us down. But when you get a little older, you realize that's not true. The organizations are ready to go to give individuals precisely what they want"

~ Steve Jobs

In this part, we will acquaint you with every one of the primary players in the current QAnon intrigue that has caught the consideration of a large portion of the United States as well as different nations all over the planet for very nearly three years.

QAnon

This the character behind an unknown source that is transformed into a developing extremist paranoid fear development in only a couple of brief years. Regardless of whether this turns out to be only one individual or a gathering of people, no one is altogether certain.

The principal "Q-Drop" occurred in October 2017 where they utilized the expression "Fleeting tranquility before all hell breaks loose." This post was agreed upon "Q Clearance Patriot." What caused many American's to sit straight up and start to pay heed to Q was that it had just been a brief time before this that President Trump had facilitated a supper for high positioning military authorities on October 5, 2017 and made reference to precisely that equivalent remark. He rehashed the expression two times during his discourse. What was additionally surprising with regards to this supper was that it was whenever that the media first had at any point been welcome to go to such an event.

It's obscure whether this is a group, an extreme male, or female. No one truly knows other than their case to have incredibly high insight leeway which is frequently alluded to as "Q-level freedom," connected to the US Department of Energy. The first posts asserted that they were near the President of the United States and there were references made to specific things that were intended to be covered up or kept hidden from the overall population. First appearing on message boards 4chan, then 8chan and Reddit's "theGreatAwakening." Despite the FBI having named these scheme scholars as a danger to public safety and basically calling them fear based oppressors, however quick as one site may be shut, another ascents in its place and the development keeps on acquiring energy (Calfas, 2017; Cassin and Wendling, 2018).

The posts uncovered by Q are very enigmatic while evening out incredibly dim charges at the very tip top and most influential people and rich families on the planet. This individual or aggregate blames these people for probably the most horrifying wrongdoings possible. Aside from talking about things that are occurring on the planet at the present time, there has all the earmarks of being an exceptional interest in Hillary Clinton as well as Robert Mueller. Others who stand out from Q have been Joe Podesta and different individuals from his family.

Another intriguing peculiarity in regards to QAnon (the Anon alluding to "Mysterious" which is in every case how these messages are posted) is that they don't have all the earmarks of being an unmistakable plan, other than to uncover defilement and halting the evil inside the dividers of the White House. Contingent upon what's going on in the magnificent universe of Q at that point, there are regularly perplexes that should be addressed. At different times they allude explicitly to influential people and give specific data. One reason we accept they are so fruitful in keeping these paranoid notions alive is on the grounds that they aren't truly taking care of data to the majority. They are leaving a path of pieces of information behind them and training individuals to look for reality themselves (Davies, 2020).

QAnon Following

The quantity of devotees that QAnon is at present getting appear to have shot this connivance scholar solidly into the spotlight. This has been a spot that Q has delighted in since that underlying post in October 2017. Posts show up regularly and regardless of how diligently anybody attempts to impede these supposed Q-Drops, they keep on showing up on the web and have been acquiring energy. Whenever asked the number of people have confidence in what Q is talking about, apparently a developing number of Americans do. They turn up at Trump rallies in large numbers and all appear to be ardent allies of what Trump is attempting to achieve.

It's not simply in America that QAnon is acquiring both after and traction.

Many of these adherents give off an impression of being renowned people who are both keen and knowledgeable. This is not something that is just going to go away because it is uncomfortable or inconvenient for people to hear what Q has to say seeing as they appear to be so radical and very clearly in support of Trump being reelected in November 2020. These allies range from renowned Hollywood stars to high-positioning government officials or those presently campaigning for office. Support for QAnon is both noticeable and expressed (Caffier, 2018).

Wikileaks and Julian Assange

It all began with a crisis call to the workplace of Hillary Clinton in 2010 by Julian Assange, the Founder of Wikileaks. Hillary Clinton was the US Secretary of State at that point and part of the Obama organization. Assange was calling to caution her that there were great many unredacted archives connecting with her office that were going to be transferred onto the Internet for all the world to see.

Assange was told to call again in a couple of hours. Notwithstanding his frantic supplications with those in the White House for the Secretary of State to accept his call expressing that individuals' lives could be in danger assuming nothing was done to forestall the hole. Further to these archives being spilled through a British and American media houses. This was only the beginning of what might eventually be her demise when it came to her bombed official mission against President Donald Trump in 2016 (BBC News US and Canada, 2016).

Bill and Hillary Clinton

Part of this paranoid notion is that Bill and Hillary Clinton are the heads of the mystery secrecy development that is essential for a youngster sex dealing ring. It's accepted that this is a Satanic development and Bill and Hillary Clinton are really at the top of this gathering of people as well as a significant number of their affluent companions and accomplices. These convictions are being energized by numerous mysterious gatherings, obscure email messages tracing all the way back to their time in the White House as well as the way that while in office as Secretary of State, Hillary wouldn't utilize her White House server for every last bit of her correspondence. All things being equal, she would utilize a private server that was hauled around with her any place she went.

These charges were made almost immediately in her residency as Secretary of State and when the Wikileaks matter was going to completely expose, Assange was attempting to caution her what was coming. Whenever he was ineffective, Hillary and her organization staff had to scramble in endeavors to annihilate proof of individual interchanges that were exceptionally dubious. At the point when "news" of this broke in the media, President Obama professed to have no information that the Secretary of State was utilizing her own private mail server.

Eventually, she had to hand it over in light of the fact that there were obviously

delicate and secret archives connecting with the American government contained among the records that she'd been speaking with people all over the planet for roughly three years after the Wikileaks episode. Her underlying reaction was to reach her lawyers and between them they annihilated in excess of 30,000 records. Questions have been raised as to what information many of these documents contained? Many of her staff at the time confirmed that President Obama had received communications from her on an ongoing basis and could obviously tell from the email address that her mails were not coming from the government server.

We will cover the various different key relationships that both Bill and Hillary Clinton have been involved in and why their names keep on being brought up as part of the current conspiracy theory that's rapidly gaining traction in the United States and around the world.

Barack Obama

Past President Barack Obama is likewise in the terminating line with large numbers of these hypotheses for quite some time. One of the first and potentially the main one is the cozy relationship divided among the Obama's and the Clinton's. Due to this affiliation, it's accepted that both Barack and Michelle Obama share in Clinton's conviction and development towards the New World Order and are additionally dynamic individuals from the secrecy. We will consider this data further in a profound jump where we examine large numbers of the exercises, activities, and significant choices made by the past President not just during his time in office as the President of the United States, however in his present limit and in his all out scorn for President Donald Trump. During this examination we will likewise uncover the job that he needed to capitalize on in Donald Trump's choice to run for President.

Donald Trump

President Donald Trump is and consistently has been a fan top pick for a decent fear inspired notion. For reasons unknown, he has been believed to be the main person who has been "distinguished" by the secretive "Q" just like the main person who has been decided to get rid of the shrewd "secrecy" and obliterate the danger that any New World Order carries with it. A significant number of the mystery and secretive messages left on different dull web talk sheets or locales are phrased so that they are favorable to Trump. For the people who attempt to go facing Trump or his chosen authorities, "Q" can be opposing. For the term of the political race of Trump in November 2020, he has been dynamic on message sheets, hauling each paranoid idea out of the book to even out the battlegrounds with his adversaries (Perez, 2020).

A free news feature from September 3, 2020 recounts the narrative of how 33% of President Donald Trump's supporters accept, or somewhat accept, in the fear inspired notions standing out as truly newsworthy at this point. Some accept that the President is engaged with a mystery battle against the barbarian pedophile sex-dealing ring known as the secrecy. In light of this, the President has affirmed that he has barely any insight into the gathering for sure they represent other than liking that they appear to like him. At the point when gotten some information about his job in attempting to stop this kid sex dealing ring, he nearly evaded around the subject by let the media know that assuming that is what they accept, he will give his all to help any place he can (Vallejo, 2020).

Joe Biden

Joe Biden was a Vice-President of the United States between 2009 to 2017 for President Obama. As an individual from the Democratic Party, he tossed his cap in the ring for the Democratic Presidential possibility to run against Donald Trump in the November 2020 general decisions. Taking everything into account, the sheer volume of those putting stock in the QAnon paranoid notions is "humiliating." He is referring to the whole fear inspired notion as "absolutely odd." During a mission discourse in Delaware, he was requested his perspective on the gathering that is intently following this paranoid fear. As indicated by Danielle Zoellner from the Independent in New York, Biden's reaction was that "the extreme right scheme bunch… ought to get a psychological well-being check… " (Rodriguez and Caputo, 2020)

President Donald Trump wouldn't remark with regards to this issue. In a similar meeting Biden calls POTUS out on the reckless idea of energizing unmerited tales that "Satan-adoring pedophiles presently run a sex dealing plot and are neutralizing the president. These devotees likewise feel that left-inclining legislators and superstars are involved." Biden calls having faith in these speculations both risky and humiliating when seen by the remainder of the world. (Zoellner, 2020).

Jeffrey Epstein and Ghislaine Maxwell

Convicted pedophile and very rich person Jeffrey Epstein was attached to sex dealing and flying little youngsters to his private island close to St. Thomas in the Caribbean. These demonstrations were supposed to be so terrible thus successive that even after his first capture and conviction he went on with this evil conduct. Shots of his island show a few sketchy designs and outfitting in shots that have been caught either loftily or by those meeting the island. Holly Aguirre from Vanity Fair consulted somebody working at the airstrip that Epstein would utilize at regular intervals to ship underage young ladies to his island. They affirmed that "specialists never really halted him. It was like he was displaying it."

Although he'd been compelled to enroll as a sex guilty party, this never really halted his conduct. Flight records that had been distributed recently demonstrated that something like one of his gulfstream jets were airborne somewhere around once at regular intervals. His objections included London, Mexico, Morocco, Paris and Slovakia. They affirmed that in every one of these examples, these planes would land close to one of their extravagance homes in either New York City or Palm Beach, Florida.

An air traffic regulator wishing to stay mysterious affirmed a few cases where Epstein would land with little youngsters who were plainly underage. This was affirmed by another air terminal worker who remarked that young ladies would frequently be wearing school pullovers to attempt to hide how youthful they truly were. They would likewise be conveying shopping packs with fashioner names like Dior and Gucci.

What aggravated matters was that he was known to be a sex

wrongdoer and gone on as though everything was all good. Flying under the radar. A portion of different things that Epstein's flight logs uncovered were the number of notable names of influential individuals had made a trip to his island. A portion of these incorporate Bill Clinton who was enrolled on flight logs as having taken roughly 26 trips on board the 727 Boeing nicknamed the "Lolita Express," all inside the space of a 2-year duration somewhere in the range of 2001 and 20013.

Ghislaine Maxwell

British socialite and long-lasting buddy of Epstein is embroiled as being intensely associated with the sex-dealing of little youngsters. This all becomes known when Virginia Roberts Giuffre records suit against both Epstein and Maxwell. She guarantees that Maxwell moved toward her when she was functioning as a youthful storage space chaperon at Donald Trump's Mar-a-Lago Club. She made guarantees of preparing her to turn into a voyaging masseuse. At the point when Giuffre demonstrates that she doesn't know anything about rub, Maxwell supposedly guarantees that all her preparation would be dealt with. This preparation, Giuffre demanded, was preparing her to be a sex-slave. She was fifteen years of age at the time.

In the ebb and flow lawful case that includes Maxwell, a large number of the records encompassing this period had been fixed because of the matter being settled. The court anyway has requested that these reports presently be unlocked and a portion of the awful demonstrations executed by Epstein show that Maxwell was a lot of a piece of the whole plan (Bekiempis, 2020).

She would apparently track down the youngsters for Epstein and among them they would move them to Epstein's private island where the young ladies would be compelled to engage in sexual relations with both Epstein and Maxwell. This was all in anticipation of them to be "pimped" out by Epstein and Maxwell to incredibly well off and high profile people including lawmakers, lawyers, and even Prince Andrew (truth be told, exactly the same Prince Andrew of the British Royals). Giuffre affirms that she had to have intercourse with the Prince something like multiple times that she could review. Naming and disgracing a portion of the people she had to have intercourse with turned out to be clear during the preliminary while she says that there were so many that everything turned into a haze in the end.

Trump Connection

Even Donald Trump is seen posturing for a photo close by Epstein in 1997 and on one more event in 2002. Trump had effectively shown that he comprehended Epstein was into a lot more youthful "ladies." Shortly before his "helpful self destruction" on August 10, 2020, Jeffrey Epstein boasted with regards to his renowned rundown of remarkable, strong, and well known people who had partaken in his sexual adventures on his private island in the Virgin Islands in the Caribbean. Trump expressed in a 2002 meeting with New York Magazine that he had known "Jeff for quite a long time. spectacular person." Trump affirms in this interview that Epstein partakes in his public activity with ladies who are a lot more youthful than him. As per Kellyann Conway who is important for President Trump's staff, he currently expresses that the activities of Epstein were "totally unseemly and clearly criminal." This was by reports from the Associated Press (Colvin, 2019).

Arrest of Epstein

Jeffrey Epstein was captured for the second time on July 6, 2019 getting back from one of his outings to France. He was blamed for attacking another little kid and during a police assault there were innumerable photos of youngsters viewed as all around his home. There would have been no chance that he would get away from genuine prison time in this occasion. The expression of a very rich person agent would never again hold facing such an immense measure of proof and this inferred that he would confront some genuine prison time. Unlike his previous arrest which was for "soliciting a prostitute" in 2005, where he only served thirteen months of an eighteen month sentence, and even this was hardly like proper jail time. During this time of imprisonment, he was permitted out six out of seven days for "work" purposes and was detained in a private wing of the jail. With the data being tossed at him, it looked like a large number of the charges would at last stick this time. Would his relationship with Bill Clinton be able to have been a danger to Hillary's expected political decision to the Presidency (Silverstein, 2015)?

Death of Jeffrey Epstein

Towards the finish of July 2019 Epstein is hospitalized for an endeavored self destruction and should be set under every minute of every day self destruction watch. On the morning of August 10, Epstein is observed dead in his cell and his demise is ascribed to self destruction. What is questionable with regards to his demise is that neither of the watchmen that should watch him are around at the hour of his passing and the cameras observing him were unexpectedly "flawed." Can anybody say "scheme?" Nobody yet the perpetrator(s) themselves could stop for a minute truly occurred in the passing of Jeffrey Epstein.

What's considerably more abnormal is that his private island is as yet under consistent gatekeeper and insurance. No one gets onto the island or off the island by any means now. Has been alluded to as "Wrongdoing Island," or

"Orgy Island" still being run by someone? Is someone still pulling the strings when it comes to the sex trafficking ring that he was running all over the world? There are many extraordinarily rich and powerful people's names and numbers that appear in what's been referred to as Jeffrey Epstein's black book.

Robert Mueller

Mueller is supposed to research one more paranoid idea that the Russians were associated with apparatus the 2016 US political decision that set President Donald Trump into his ebb and flow position. As indicated by Q, this "supposed examination" isn't correct. They guarantee that Mueller and Trump are cooperating researching Hillary Clinton, Barack Obama, and Joe Podesta. Every one of the three should have a place with the secrecy and are important for the "covert government" that POTUS continues to allude to.

Other Players on the Board

Q ensnares the Illuminati, normal characters in paranoid fears who are constantly associated with anything detestable that is happened throughout history. These occasions, in these hypotheses, would tie back to either the Illuminati or the Freemasons. They denounce numerous other mega affluent world class people as being important for pedophile rings, part of Satanic religions and other shocking developments that are planning to do evil. QAnon appears to dislike any individual or association that takes steps to change the world in a negative manner. Alluding straightforwardly to keeping the New World Order from occurring, there is an unmistakable sign that Q is against any of the socially tip top and anticipates freeing the universe of debasement and insidiousness. As per Q, these disasters in all actuality do truth be told exist on the planet and the Illuminati are out there alongside other mystery associations like the Masonic Order.

Chapter 4: Pizzagate

"There is a clique of obliviousness in the United States and there has been all the time. Yet again the strain of hostile to intellectualism has been a consistent clear a path through our political and social life, sustained by the

misleading idea that majority rules government implies that my obliviousness is similarly pretty much as great as your knowledge"

~ Isaac Asimov

Podesta Leaks

As Hillary Clinton approaches the finish of her 2016 political race, WikiLeaks starts delivering a constant flow of hacked archives associated with her and her reasonableness as official competitor. The residue has barely settled with respect to the private server occurrence where Hillary and co are unequivocally reprimanded by the FBI in regards to her all out negligence for touchy government data. For her whole term in office as the Secretary of State, Ms. Clinton and her staff worked by something else altogether of rules. Decides that applied to any remaining individuals from staff under the Obama organization were just mocked by the State department.

Citing that it was "inconvenient' carrying multiple devices and servers etc. on her travels, she chose to go with her private server instead. This was a hot potato that nobody wanted to handle. We discussed how the owner of WikiLeaks, Julian Assange, tried to warn Ms. Clinton that unredacted documents were about to be leaked all over the internet and her subsequent scramble to delete more than 30,000 personal emails with the help of her attorneys. How does one individual justify more than 30,000 pieces of information needed to be deleted? The questions remain as to what was so important that needed to be hidden.

Having quite recently endure her own adventure, to be confronted with another dirty move in regards to hacked messages, this time having a place with her mission director, Joe Podesta.

What the greater part of these reports plainly demonstrated was the specific power that

little gatherings of Democrats had in pushing the wheels of government ahead and guiding it as they saw fit. Many messages depended on nepotism or endeavored nepotism, who knew who, who needed what work and each and every individual who was anybody connected with Joe Podesta. A significant number of these messages showed that Joe Podesta was the individual to address to invest energy at the first class or elitist setting Martha's Vineyard. This was generally simply presented out to top legislators and those nearest to POTUS. For reasons unknown, people were reaching Joe

Podesta about these sorts of requests.

These were not just legislators who appeared to show up in his range of prominence by numerous other well known people from creators to celebrities. If you didn't have Joe Podesta's email, then you clearly weren't in the know or could not be classified as being well connected on the Hill. What's important to understand about Joe Podesta is that he had been in positions of power for decades and was extremely well connected. At the time the Podesta messages started to spill there were various people who cried "foul" and inferred that the sends were adulterated and that Podesta was just a substitute for the Democrats, at this point under a lot nearer examination they gave off an impression of being genuine.

Pizzagate Takes Root

So, we should get to how the whole pizzagate adventure unfurled. Among all the Podesta spilled messages were numerous mysterious messages that were shipped off different people and interchanges appeared to be continuous for a long time. These messages alluded to "pizza" as well as "pasta" with different fixings. While we can't verify or refute whether or not any of these messages were authentic (recall that I said toward the start of this book that a portion of this data planned to get a piece rushed), this is one of those spots. What these obscure messages inferred or were "translated" to suggest is that "pasta" was alluding to "little youngsters" while "pizza" was alluding to "young men." The unique "fixings" alluded to anything the person who was keen on securing these kids needed to do with them.

Suddenly Q-Drops started getting on this and evidently unraveled these messages to embroil Joe Podesta as a component of a kid sex-dealing ring and that

there were people and gatherings of people who were associated with the most shocking of violations against small kids. Some way or another, when this data was gotten and deciphered by QAnon, it was suggested that there were some high-positioning lawmakers and other political figures who were engaged with this pedophile and youngster sex-dealing ring. Devotees of QAnon started after the Q-Drops in regards to profound implications in the "pizza" emails.

Some of these messages alluded to a famous pizza eatery in the D.C. region. This episode before long becomes known as "Pizzagate." It's only one occurrence where one of QAnon's devotees take an extreme position against "the foundation" in the desire for uncovering the debasement that is plainly apparent in the messages that are being spilled by WikiLeaks.

Those after the pizzagate Q-Drops had confidence in the evil secrecy of pedophiles working out of Comet Ping Pong, yet they trusted that the proprietor of the eatery, James Alefantis, was a lot of a piece of dealing these kids. Anyway, how did Comet Ping Pong turn into the focal point of the discussion? When some of Joe Podesta's messages were hacked, obviously there were a great deal of messages between James Alefantis and Podesta. A portion of the messages allude to the eatery potentially facilitating a pledge drive for Hillary Clinton.

At the time, messages started springing up on 4chan which was the message load up that QAnon was utilizing at that point. There started to be theory that the dealing ring was the thing was occurring out of Comet Ping Pong. It was generally guiltless until somebody on 4chan posted that they had "proof" that this was going on at Comet Ping Pong. One of the principle justifications for why this café became designated was on the grounds that it was "kid well disposed" and offered a lot of games and exercises for the children to do, from ping-pong tables (consequently the name) to rooms devoted to makes. As a craftsman and genuine Clinton ally, Alefantis knew both Joe Podesta and his sibling, Tony Podesta, who both used to visit the café on a standard basis.

Shortly before the underlying assault on the eatery, Alefantis and a significant number of his staff started getting undermining messages and calls at the café as well as via web-based media. Pictures of youngsters that were taken at the eatery were duplicated from their site and it was suggested that these were verification that they were truth be told working a kid sex-dealing ring out of the

café. At the point when individuals started showing up at the eatery to "see with their own eyes," Alefantis carved out it was opportunity to connect with both the police and the FBI to aid the matter as it had now obviously turned all the way out of control.

Throughout the days following the 2016 political decision, some genuine conservative revolutionaries started voicing their own viewpoints with regards to this issue, causing some serious problems until it became inconceivable for anybody following these strings on 4chan to ignore.

What's muCh more strange was that knowledgeable and well-expecting people really started trusting these loads up and on the grounds that it appeared like no one was making any move at that point, he concluded that as a parent and concerned resident, it was his obligation to liberate the youngsters from this savage mystery secrecy working inside the American government. One of these QAnon enthusiasts, 28-year-old Edgar Maddison Welch, settled on the morning of December 4, 2016 that he'd had pretty much had enough of the relative multitude of posts with respect to pedophilia and maltreatment of youngsters by these high-profile government officials. He chose to get in his vehicle in North Carolina and travel many miles to Washington D.C. to the pizza restaurant.

Climbing out of his vehicle, Welch starts shooting up the spot with an attack rifle, raging a café that is practically filled and requests to see the "storm cellar" where the Satanic formal maltreatment and penance of these kids should be occurring. Luckily for Welch, no one was harmed during his arbitrary shootout. He before long finds that this well known family eatery has no cellar and gives up to police the second they show up. Welch is captured possessing an attack rifle, a handgun, another shotgun, and a collapsing blade. What might he have done assuming he found the notorious eatery had a basement?

Although Welch is captured in a profoundly pitched activity, this doesn't stop extreme traditional people and other "concerned residents" from focusing on the café. Ryan Jaselskis sets one of their draperies land in 2019, is captured, and condemned to four years in jail despite the fact that he experiences a state of mind (Sebastian, 2016).

False Flags

For the individuals who have never heard this wording truly being utilized, its underlying foundations are profoundly saturated with old customs when privateers used to cruise the high oceans. What might frequently happen is privateer boats would regularly fly "well disposed" banners having a place with nations for the purpose of drawing nearer to their primary targets (other nautical vessels). When sufficiently close, they would load up the contrary vessel and either assume responsibility for the boat, plunder it of every one of its substance, take detainees, or do whatever was of most noteworthy advantage to the privateers at that point. This term is utilized when any "redirection" strategy is utilized for of drawing your consideration starting with one circumstance then onto the next, regardless of how short the period. It's intended to make you glance one way while something different totally unique is going on some place else.

Surprisingly for such an old practice, it is still especially alive and happening from one side of the planet to the other even as you read this.

Members of the Trump organization including Michael Flynn Jr. kept on tweeting that the raging of Comet Ping Pong was a bogus banner and was planned to offer help for the media to start blue penciling content. Different individuals from the Trump organization kept defaming Hillary Clinton by means of Twitter in regards to the utilization of the private server and her 30,000 records that bafflingly vanished.

Where's Pizzagate today?

So, the first pizzagate was apparently gobbled up in the principle QAnon fear inspired notion [that President Donald Trump is here to save the world from the covert government secrecy that are furtively eating children]. Yet again while a large portion of Trump's more seasoned allies appeared to be content to leave the pizza on the plate, in 2020, it appears to have popped up and this time with a lot more youthful gathering of people. The TikTok age. The players on the board have additionally changed. The youngster sex-dealers have now been focused on Ellen DeGeneres and Chrissy Teigen. The Wayfair brand has likewise been tossed in with the general mish-mash. You might be asking how in the world Wayfair has gotten themselves involved in this embarrassment? Indeed, incidentally, the name Waif and admission were separated and turned upward on the Merriam-Webster word reference. Since it evidently alludes to transportation and young ladies, someone has locked onto this and chosen on the grounds that Ellen DeGeneres is in organization with the organization that she's in some way associated with these scandals.

Although there have been a huge number of QAnon sites that have been impeded, exiled, banned, or "cleansed" between Reddit, Twitter and various other web-based media locales somewhere in the range of 2016 and 2020, there simply is by all accounts no shutting down these rumors.

Calm Before the Storm

On the evening of October 6, 2017, President Trump engaged top military faculty and their accomplices at a supper. Unexpectedly, the press and media are welcome to go to this supper. During a photograph an open door with everybody, the President cites that this "might be the fleeting tranquility before all hell breaks loose, it's the fleeting tranquility before all hell breaks loose!" When squeezed by the media regarding what he implied by this assertion, he declines to reply. The main thing the media escapes him further is a wink and a "pensive!" He recognizes that a portion of the world's most impressive military personalities turned out to be available and in the room at the time.

The extremely following day, POTUS retweets what was shipped off him by Republican contender for Georgia, Angela Stanton King, "THE STORM IS HERE." This was one of a few retweets from QAnon on the side of the President's remarks from the supper held the past evening. As per those supporting QAnon, the tempest that the President was alluding to his goal of "cleaning house" and uncovering the debasement and evil inside the abnormal and degenerate government officials in the White House and every one of their comrades. Likewise with any great paranoid fear, no proof that any moves are is being made by President Trump or any other person besides with regards to uncovering defilement from inside the dividers of the White House (Brewster, 2020).

Naturally, this adds extra fuel to an all around seething fire and the FBI starts to caution of the risks of extreme right extreme radicals. They are making an honest effort to target and get rid of any individual who is by all accounts following QAnon and some other scheme scholar bunches out there. Not having an excessive amount of progress I could add. In a tweet from Stanton King on August 5, 2020 she

remarks "I haven't had the option to arrange Pizza. Much appreciated, pedos." While this barely appears to be suitable for an administration official to tweet or retweeting about, apparently Stanton King is an enthusiastic QAnon adherent and ally notwithstanding denying this on various events. She has frequently utilized the QAnon hashtag #WWG1WGA (where we go one, we go all).

Where We Go One, We Go All

"Where we go one, we go all" has turned into the hashtag handle for QAnon adherents everywhere. Albeit many have credited this statement to the late president John F. Kennedy, it's really a statement from the 1996 film, White Squall. The person Chuck Gieg played by Scott Wolf statements the line: "You let us know where we go one we go all, well we accepted you, we resided by it, Sir. Also currently you're saying where you go we can't follow." Just to explain for those out there accepting that they were truth be told after a connivance scholar who was citing past presidents (Wessel, 1996).

Although the film depends on the recorded sinking of a twin pole transport, the Albatross that was annihilated in a white gust in 1961. Could this be the references that Q keeps on referring to as "THE STORM IS HERE?" One of the few survivors of this event confirmed at the time the movie was released that the storm appeared out of nowhere and disappeared as quickly as it had appeared. Had it not been for the sinking of the vessel in under five minutes, no one would have been any the wiser.

Continuous Media Coverage

While many accept that providing details regarding QAnon is crazy and all exposure should be halted, colleague teacher of correspondence at Syracuse University, Whitney Phillips accepts that they are drawing in more adherents. Phillips expressed that media not covering QAnon happenings would additionally add to the paranoid ideas out there. She warns that even attempting to debunk QAnon through media coverage can give whoever QAnon is the credibility necessary to gain further traction. As an expert in correspondences, she affirms that whoever is behind the QAnon trick is as of now adoring the consideration that they're getting from the media.

Breadcrumbs, Breads and Bakers

The first posts from Q were posted on the dim web on a board known as 4chan. The references to breadcrumbs, breads, and dough punchers connect with how the 4chan webpage functions and its web represent those up to date and experts in everything that are PC and web related. Unique posts are known as bread. Strings that create because of the first post are alluded to as breadcrumbs and the people who are presenting them or answering on them are alluded to as the dough punchers. There have been a few fascinating examinations directed by various understudies who were given precisely a one month window to research all that they could with respect to QAnon on 4chan, how the "person" really transformed into a group, leaving them doubting whether the first Q was even accountable for the posts any longer. By figuring out their information, apparently they distinguished the unique wellspring of QAnon as first showing up on 4chan on October 27, 2017. Their review comprised of attempting to follow every one of these strings through logical means between November 1, 2017 and December 1, 2017 (Kir et. Al., 2020).

Chapter 5: The Controversial Clintons

"First rule of progress is debate. You can't move away from it for the straightforward explanation all issues are dubious. Change implies development, and development implies grating, and contact implies

hotness, and hotness implies controversy."

~ Saul Alinsky

Controversy appears to conceal Bill and Hillary Clinton any place they go. From the time he became President of the United States in 1993, there have been outrages related with both him and his better half Hillary Rodham Clinton. Anything the justification for the total scorn that QAnon has for the Clinton's this stays muddled. A portion of the principal Q-Drops turned out to foresee that "HRC was going to be captured." In this occurrence, the "HRC" alludes to Hillary Rodham Clinton.

Those after the start of these strings held up in expectation, expecting for the news to be land with the capture of Hillary Clinton. Obviously, nothing occurred. All things considered, she is under house capture and is donning one of those trendy lower leg screens that will not permit her to get much of anywhere except if she is under close security. No one has seen her wearing a lower leg screen, so this simply adds to the demeanor of secret encompassing the paranoid fear of her arrest.

This isn't to say that there are no obvious explanations to be careful about the Clintons. They have been associated with a few obscure dealings since prior to going into the White House back in 1993. How about we take a gander at one of the main outrages they became engaged with not long after moving into the White House.

Travelgate – 1993

The Clintons had no sooner moved into the White House when it was becoming extremely evident to many of the White House staff that they would have another Eleanor Roosevelt on their hands if Hillary Clinton was allowed to get her way. From the get-go in her significant other's initial term in office, she

became displeased and grumbled about not having sufficient say in the "recruiting and terminating" of people on the President's staff. This prompted what might become known as the "Travelgate outrage." In May 1993, President Bill Clinton and First Lady Hillary Rodham Clinton chose to terminate seven representatives from the Travel Department in the White House.

Reasons for excusing these workers were refered to as monetary mistakes (which were totally unwarranted). The staff were terminated to clear a path for companions of the First Lady's to take up these situations in the White House. To place this into point of view, working in the Travel Department for the President implied admittance to travel all around the world as well as extremely liberal pay rates and advantages. At that point, a staff of seven people had a working spending plan of roughly US $7 million each year.

A close companion of the First Lady who claimed a legitimate travel service in Arkansas by the name of World Wide Travel was designated by the First Lady to deal with all White House travel courses of action. It's likewise accepted that a portion of the positions were filled by far off family members of the Clinton family.

Hollywood maker, Harry Thomason, and his accomplice, Darnell Martens supplanted the Airline of America sanction administration that had been utilized by the White House for a long time. Under the flag of a business called TRM, they just worked for the white house in 1992 and were granted an airplane contract review esteemed at $500,000.

Investigations into this single occurrence happened for a long time somewhere in the range of 1993 and 2000. In January 1996, a two-year-old reminder surfaced that should be between two White House helpers. The reminder straightforwardly alludes to what in particular would occur assuming the desires with respect to the excusals by the First Lady were not met "swiftly."

Bill Clinton

For anybody who may not know about the historical backdrop of previous President Bill Clinton, he was embroiled in various sex embarrassments. The most renowned of these was the issue with a White House assistant, Monica Lewinsky. This single issue was practically to the point of driving him out of the White House and

office as POTUS. All through his term in office, there were four different ladies who ventured forward and conceded to consensual extramarital undertakings with the President. It was only after Kathleen Willey in a meeting with Sean Hannity, Fox News have in October 2016 offered the accompanying expressions, "Everyone in the predominant media is calling all of Bill Clinton's violations treacheries... Rape, rape, and lewd behavior are not disloyalties. They are wrongdoings and they are crimes." The cases against Clinton are recorded as follows:

Juanita Broaddrick

Dating back to 1978 when Bill Clinton was still the Attorney General in Arkansas, it turns out that he brutally raped her during one of his campaign visits to Little Rock. She was just 35 years of age at that point and tells how the then Attorney General showed positively no regret or compassion towards his activities. As indicated by Broaddrick, this appeared to be being something an ordinary event for him. While no move was made against the Attorney General at that point, Juanita Broaddrick imparted her story to a dear companion following the occurrence. She substantiated the story later in court.

Kathleen Willey

No sooner had Clinton been chosen President when he's denounced by a volunteer working in the White House at that point, Kathleen Willey, of him "kissing her, [fondling] her bosoms and being compelled to contact his groin during a gathering in the Oval Office". This occurred back in 1993. Albeit these allegations were unveiled in 1998, the President level out denied them. He conceded that he could have "embraced her during this gathering and kissed her on the forehead."

They had at first been companions before this occurrence and Willey trusted in the President that they were encountering monetary hardships at that point. She found out if it very well may be workable for her volunteer situation to turn into a long-lasting one. The President's reaction to this was to demand a "private gathering" with her in a room off the Oval Office. It was here that he cornered her and physically manhandled her. During her 2016 meeting with Sean Hannity of Fox News, she transfers the story and lets him know that while all of this was going on to her, she wasn't certain about whether she should slap him, knee him in the crotch or shout for help. All that she envisioned was the mystery administration racing to the guide of the President and having firearms to her head, so all things considered she did nothing.

Paula Jones

Still during his tenure as Governor of Arkansas Bill Clinton used his position of power to arrange for the police to bring Paula Jones to his hotel room. In this gathering he dropped his jeans, uncovering all that he'd been brought into the world with and propositioned her for sex. Whenever she informed him that she "wasn't that sort of young lady," he encouraged all her it between them. Jones unveiled her claims in 1994, soon after Clinton was chosen President. Albeit the adjudicator excused the charges in 1998 on the premise that neither Jones nor her standing had been discolored by the occurrence, Clinton privately addressed any remaining issues as much as $850,000. He never conceded culpability or apologized for his actions.

Leslie Millwee

Once the real truth was out in the open and this multitude of ladies started approaching blaming the President for lewd behavior, assault, and different things, Leslie Millwee includes her own story. Just uncovering the story in 2016, she guarantees that back in 1980, Bill Clinton had grabbed her at the TV slot where she worked at that point. In every one of the three separate occurrences, she had requested that he quit, letting him know that she didn't need it. She tells the story saying that he would simply carry on until he had a climax and would snicker at her. She never revealed him at the time since he was the Attorney General and stood firm on a foothold of force. She expected that it would be her statement against his. With regards to sexual charges against Bill Clinton, who can say for sure what might have surfaced because of his affectionate kinship with Jeffrey Epstein (Relman, 2017)?

In every one of the above occurrences when faced, we observe that Bill Clinton lies right out of each and every situation. Maybe it's the pathological lies that QAnon has against the Clinton Clan? Both the ex-President and ex-Presidential Candidate have been discovered in lies while under oath for numerous allegations from scandals in the White House to many of the documents disappearing from the private server that Ms. Clinton was using.

Leaders of the Cabal

Is there any wonder why QAnon has identified them as being the leaders of this evil cabal that is threatening to take over the world and usher in a New World Order? Two things that we do know for certain about Bill Clinton is that not only did he become a member of a freemasonry order, The Order of DeMolay while he was more youthful. (Morris, 2013). Charge Clinton was additionally made an individual from the mysterious society, the Bilderberg Group, in 1991 preceding he became President of the United States, and extremist free-thinking Hillary Clinton turned into an individual from the Group from 1997. (Sandburn, 2016).

It's been hypothesized for quite a long time that this gathering is really the Cabal and due to the mystery encompassing the prominent and strong individuals from the gathering from around the globe, this probably won't be such a long ways misguided. The Bilderberg Group has been related with popular family names like the Rockefellers, Prince Edward and Prince Phillip of the Royal family, Margaret Thatcher, Tony Blair, Jeff Bezos, Bill Gates, and some more. The group consists of major players from most countries around the world who are in positions of power politically, those within academia, high-powered media moguls, key military officials, those within financial institutions, and major corporations.

Everything about these gatherings that occur yearly throughout a few days all at once occurs in secret. No minutes are taken of these gatherings and after joining, every part makes a solemn vow to mystery with respect to all that is talked about at these gatherings. This sounds increasingly more like a plot for global control than anything more. If the Bilderberg Group were nothing more than a global "think tank" as it professes to be, then surely, they would only be happy to share their knowledge with the world without fear.

The Private Server and 30,000 Emails

For the whole length of her term in office as US Secretary of State, Hillary Clinton wouldn't utilize the public authority server of some other electronic gadget like a cell phone. Expressing that it was "decidedly a lot of work changing out servers or conveying two servers with her any place she went" as a reason, she depended on involving a private server which thus would send and

get some very exceptionally grouped data. At the point when this at long last became known during the Julian Assange WikiLeaks adventure (where her office had been cautioned that the hole was coming), there was a frenzied scramble by her whole organization as well as her legitimate group to "dispose of" around 30,000 documents.

Claiming that these reports were of an individual sort and had nothing to do with her job as Secretary of State, these archives were obliterated in a short space of time. Nearly 55,000 reports were spilled in 2016 that were said to have come from Hillary Clinton's private server. Erasing 33,000 of these leaves just 22,000, way less messages than she decided to erase. How can it be to create 33,000 extra messages or private records when you're really expected to be working for the State Department? When asked straight by Donald Trump during one of their discussions before the 2017 political decision, Hillary redirected the inquiry and declined to respond to. For anybody, this absolutely causes a person to show up more blameworthy than guiltless (D. Smith, 2016).

The FBI had explored the episode and albeit all that Hillary Clinton had done to "filter" through her messages was to look through business related subjects, shippers, and regardless of whether messages had a .gov or .mil expansion at the back, this was the manner by which they arrived at the resolution that the 30,000 messages were not business related. Did the FBI go through these messages? They were told to erase them by FBI chief James Comey. Everything that was expressed with regards to the matter was "Please accept my apologies, I committed an error." Questions have since been raised whether there was a conscious goal with respect to Hillary and her lawyers to erase implicating proof and messages connecting with the Benghazi assault, to which Comey answered that he questioned it had been done purposefully. Trump's require her to deliver the 33,000 has gone unanswered and unactioned (Levine, 2016).

Death of Vince Foster

There have been numerous theories encompassing the demise of Vincent Walker Foster Jr., known as Vince. Qualified as a lawyer, Foster had moved gradually up through the positions and was elevated to Deputy White House Counsel

during the initial a half year of the Clinton Administration. Attempting to unwind the paranoid notion, Vince Foster was associated with the Travelgate outrage examined above, where he expected to give direction to the President that he and the First Lady had the option to recruit and fire as they needed. The announced story is that inside the initial a half year of working at the White House under President Clinton, Vince turned out to be increasingly discouraged and was at last found dead in July 1993 in Fort Marcy Park from a shot wound.

Although five free examinations managed his passing a self destruction, there have been numerous fear inspired notions that have since surfaced that conceivably show that there was something else to Foster's demise besides met the eye. Before we can see how Vince Foster was involved, it's essential to comprehend his relationship with the Whitewater Scandal.

One of the speculations emerged from reports connecting with Whitewater that had strangely disappeared from Foster's documents following his demise and had then been found in the ownership of Clinton's lawyer. At the hour of his passing, it was accounted for that there "was light hair and floor covering filaments on his suit coat as well as semen in his clothing." This is accounted for to Salon magazine by Dan Moldea. Wrongdoing journalist Dan Moldea considered the alleged Vince Foster self destruction for a very long time since there were irregularities found in the investigation.

Some super conservatives got hold of this data and out of nowhere there were films seeming declaring that the Clintons were some way or another engaged with his passing and that it was anything but a self destruction as initially announced. The recreation area police, Major Robert Hines, affirms with two separate media houses, Christopher Ruddy of the New York Post, and Reed Irvine of Accuracy in Media that there was no leave wound. As a result of these remarks, Moldea kept delving into the passing of Vince Foster. Many felt that his self destruction had been arranged to resemble a self destruction with the weapon being put in his grasp after he'd been shot. They additionally accept that his body had been moved to give the presence of self destruction. Whenever Irvine and Ruddy squeezed Hines for what he implied by "there was no leave wound," he remedied his underlying explanations saying that he needed to offer a remark to the media at the time.

Whitewater Scandal

Whitewater should be an ocean front advancement along the White River in Arkansas. The Clintons became associated with Jim and Susan McDougal, some long-lasting companions who had practical experience in land. The Whitewater Development Corporation was framed in 1979 between the Clinton's and the Mcdougal's. The McDougal's additionally ended up claiming a financing association, Madison Guaranty Savings and Loan, which would propose to help people wishing to put resources into the Whitewater property development.

By the time legal actions were brought against the McDougal's and the Clinton's, the Clinton's inexplicably gotten away from any contribution in the plan. Susan McDougal was condemned to eighteen months for scorn of court as she would not address any inquiries with respect to Whitewater. She just served thirteen months of prison time and was exculpated by President Clinton instantly before he left office in 2000.

Murder of Seth Rich

Another inexpliCable homiciDe secret encompassing one of the Democratic Party individuals from staff, Seth Rich. This murder was first answered to be crafted by Hillary Clinton by Fox News. The asAll in allciation evidently in counter for the WikiLeaked archives on the server of Hillary Clinton during her Presidential mission in 2016. So, what befell Seth Rich? Seth Rich was a brilliant 27-year-old individual from the Democratic Committee. At roughly 4:20 am, Rich was gunned down two times in the back by obscure aggressors in Bloomingdale, D.C. The conventional report from the police guarantee that it was a bungled endeavored robbery.

While nothing could be demonstrated and his demise stays a secret, some conservatives by and by started pointing their fingers at Hillary Clinton. Seth Rich had been denounced similar to the justification for the reports spilling to WikiLeaks, albeit this was subsequently ended up being created. It's far-fetched that we will at any point truly realize what occurred with Seth Rich in the early hours of

that Sunday morning. Nothing was taken and he never saw the culprits since he was shot toward the back. It's far-fetched that reality will at any point come out.

Suicide of Jeffrey Epstein

Yet another dubious "self destruction" that has been connected to the Clinton's is that of extremely rich perAll in alln agent, Jeffrey Epstein. Paul Gosar, a Republican from Arizona tweeted multiple times that "EPSTEIN DID NOT KILL HIMSELF." Unlike QAnon, Gosar made plainly this was what he accepted, notwithstanding attempting to retreat asserting that he didn't intend to suggest that Epstein had been killed by somebody. So, what was he attempting to say? Epstein was as yet alive? This is one more fear inspired notion completely all alone. While the New York City clinical analyst affirmed demise by self destruction, a second free clinical inspector recruited by Epstein's sibling questioned the discoveries of the NYC ME.

So, the talk plant started with respect to how Epstein truly passed on. We've effectively referenced over that there are portions of this case that really warrant profound examination. Epstein ought not have been separated from everyone else, and for what reason were the camera's not working during his genuine self destruction? Not even Epstein would have had the option to organize all of that himself, and assuming he was so discouraged and self-destructive, how is it that he could have even devised such an accursed plan to start with?

It doesn't take long for President Trump to commit to this paranoid fear (recall that we've referenced the amount he flourishes with deception and partakes in an old fashioned paranoid notion). Not long after Epstein's demise, he delivered a recording where he "guesses" over who's liable for Epstein's passing and afterward the hashtags start...
#ClintonBodyCount and #ClintonCrimefamily. While Gosar had just implied that there had been another side to this alleged self destruction than was being delivered to general society, POTUS clarified who he believed was responsible.

Possible Reasons for Wanting Epstein Dead

You might be asking what reasons the Clinton's might have for needing to keep Jeffrey Epstein calm. Several reasons come into view. In the first place, given the proclivities of Bill Clinton who had been "surprised" more regularly than one would mind to specify. Clinton was a "regular customer" on the Lolita Express and invested a great deal of energy with Jeffrey Epstein on his island and voyaged broadly with him.

When Epstein was first captured and the police found all the visual proof of Epstein with the youngsters, Bill Clinton was involved similar to a major piece of this sex-dealing ring. While it was still up in the air regarding his genuine contribution, it's accepted that there are many implicating photos of Bill Clinton with a portion of the "stock." Reasons for needing to keep their names out of any relationship with the disasters and abominations of Jeffrey Epstein would be reason to the point of needing to dispose of him before he had to testify.

Bill and Hillary Clinton's names appeared in Epstein's black book and it was believed that Bill Clinton flew with Epstein a couple of times to Africa, and to Europe and Asia. According to Bill Clinton, the only reason he was friends with Epstein in the first place was "because he owned a plane." Once again, Bill Clinton emphatically denies ever having been to Little St. James Island (Giuffre confirms that at least one of the times she was there, Bill Clinton was there.) Remember, both he and Hillary lied under oath. Bill Clinton had already been accused of raping Juanita Broaddrick and from her testimony, so it wasn't far-fetched to believe that he might make full use of all the services Epstein was providing. (Matthews, 2019)

Clinton Foundation

This family establishment was established in 1997 under Bill Clinton's name. The alleged general reason for the establishment is that it is a non-benefit, charge absolved and intended to "fortify the limit of individuals in the United States and all through the world to address the difficulties of worldwide interdependence."

This was one more questionable association right now shown full an ideal opportunity to Bill and Hillary Clinton. Charge Clinton has been effectively involved since he stepped

down as President of the US. Hillary additionally got out of her job as Secretary of State into the current job under the flag of their establishment. In 2016 alone, it's accepted that the establishment got roughly $2 billion in gifts from rich advocates, political gatherings, and unfamiliar state run administrations.

Many have blamed the Clinton's for inappropriateness with respect to tolerating installments as a trade-off for visitor talking tasks. It's been accounted for that a large number of these discussions go for roughly $250,000 a period. What exacerbates the situation is that there are state run administrations and private enterprises out there who will pay that sort of cash for these two people to talk! (Stracqualursi, 2020)

Chapter 6: Obama

"At times it is said that man can't be entrusted with the public authority of himself. Would he be able to then be entrusted with the public authority of others? Or then again have we tracked down heavenly messengers as rulers to oversee him? Allow history to answer this question"

~ Thomas Jefferson

The Original Trump Snub

A solitary occasion reversed the situation totally and changed the direction of the American bid for the 2016 General Elections. This occasion was the Annual White House Correspondents' Association Dinner held in 2011. A columnist for the New Yorker, Adam Gopnik, reviews the appearance of sheer fury on the essence of Donald Trump as the then President of the

United States, Barack Obama, assaulted Donald Trump's personality a large number of times offering mean remarks and telling wisecracks regarding what the White House would resemble under the tycoon's influence. He derides his TV program, "The Apprentice" and how Trump appreciates and even trusts some paranoid notions. For Gopnik it became clear from the undeniable gaze of Donald Trump, jaw grasped, showing only contempt for Obama. This single occasion adjusted the whole direction of American history.

Donald Trump had no aim of running for President of the United States at that point. In spite of the fact that he had tossed his cap in the ring two or multiple times previously, at the hour of this supper, he was not in the race for the Presidency and had recently embraced Mitt Romney. Donald Trump was effective by his own doing, a tycoon with a very sizable amount of happening in the realm of land. After this supper be that as it may, he basically would not stand around and permit Obama to criticize him further. Not before the media, and unquestionably not before a considerable lot of his companions. Retribution can be a strong weapon with regards to battling for what you need. Donald Trump knows precisely how to play the power game too and this single occasion was the tipping point where Donald Trump would choose to run for President (Gopnik, 2015).

Created ISIS with Hillary Clinton

In August of 2016, Donald Trump was consulted by Hugh Hewitt on public TV. The understanding that Hewitt provides for Trump is that Trump accepts Obama is answerable for the breakdown of harmony in the Middle East. Donald Trump passionately denies these cases. He proceeds to let Hewitt know that both Hillary Clinton and Barack Obama were the real authors of the Islamic State of Iraq and Syria (ISIS). You might be inquiring as to why this paranoid idea is as yet proceeding to acquire foothold among standard Americans and not on the money wing radicals? (Drabold, 2016)

Clint Watts, a long serving individual from the FBI's counterintelligence unit and creator of Messing With the Enemy*: Surviving in a Social Media World of Hackers, Terrorists, Russians, and Fake News was as of late evaluated by Mike Pesca from SLATE.* He remarks on how the QAnon peculiarity is continually moving and changing conviction frameworks inside numerous Americans. In spite of numerous distinctions between the QAnon gathering of devotees and those supporting ISIS, he guarantees that there are matches that could likewise be drawn,

cautioning that should there be a proportionate measure of QAnon adherents as of late and here are a portion of the things he needed to say about the possible risks of those after QAnon down the dark hole (Pesca, 2020).

Watts reminds Pesca that the government election is about to happen and warns that some of the individuals who are avid followers of QAnon and believe in all the conspiracy theories that are being spread could easily be elected to Congress. He sets the subject of what the new legislature of the US could resemble assuming this occurs. He likewise remarks about the distinction between "ordinary" paranoid ideas and the way that QAnon continues acquiring footing instead of ceasing to exist, evening following three years. Watts cautions that a portion of the supporters of QAnon could be incredibly hazardous while others follow the message sheets out of unadulterated interest. What he notes notwithstanding, is that one single scheme scholar has had the option to catch the consideration of a whole country and hold it for so long. That panics him coming from his counterterrorism foundation (Pesca, 2020).

There are a couple of fierce breakouts starting to occur on one side, while Republicans are starting to win in specific districts that don't follow normal examples of political decision hacking or altering. Watts makes a correlation with his years in counterterrorism in the FBI, while being mindful so as not to point any fingers toward QAnon or the gathering's adherents. He's alluding to the 1990s and 2000s when America wasn't certain about whether the adversary was al-Qaida or Islam. There was a great deal of time spent at the antiterrorism research focus attempting to distinguish the distinctions between these associations and what put every one aside. The principle objective was to isolate those that represented a danger and were causing viciousness versus the individuals who weren't. The FBI wasn't keen on pursuing down people who were innocuous in after their conviction system(s).

Pulling the discussion back to the current circumstance with QAnon, he contrasted it and a tapered shape. On the edges of the cone, you had the people who were basically inquisitive and were really innocuous, while the further you got into the cone, the less people were found towards the essential issue, yet these were the people who were revolutionaries. They would be the ones committed to the reason 100%. They would spew the data to everybody. They were the gathering that was to a greater extent a danger both inside and without as opposed to any other individual (Pesca, 2020).

It would be these revolutionaries who felt that they'd need to substantiate themselves deserving of being alluded to as a disciple to the reason. In the event that this implied murder and disorder, so be it, they were completely dedicated. The radicals would be less in number than the normal standard adherent, yet these were the people that the FBI was attempting to caution general Americans concerning when they've marked QAnon and all the paranoid notions that show up with it as hazardous and a potential psychological oppressor danger to the American public. For Watts, it was just a question of these extreme people "going to brutality in light of a deception framework" (Pesca, 2020).

Muslim Roots Claim

Obama stands out as truly newsworthy again while meeting the King of Saudi Arabia and bowing to him at this gathering. Once more indeed tattle starts to develop and estimate that Obama has Muslim roots in light of the fact that no different US President sane would break convention like this.

It then turns out that during his term in office as President of the United States, Obama happened to make this same mistake on a number of different occasions, for pure entertainment value, here are individuals or things that the most powerful president in the world believed to be more important than him:

- In April 2014, he was shot bowing to a Japanese robot.
- Media all through the US had an Obama taking care of free for all as he met the Saudi King during a G-20 culmination meeting.
- Recorded during a similar excursion (G-20 gathering, Obama doesn't frustrate by bowing to the Queen of England.
- One might say that during his previous years as POTUS he truly didn't have the foggiest idea about any better, in 2009 he was caught bowing to the Emperor of Japan.
- 2010 sees him bowing again to the Chinese.
- There are a few other stupid mistakes made by Obama all through his organization with regards to getting a straightforward hello right. All things considered, the President doesn't bow!

  If he quits a bow all alone, not joined by a handshake or a twofold hand hold as Obama was so enamored with doing. From bowing to a Japanese kid's lifelike model during a visit to Japan, to bowing to the city hall leader of Tampa, Florida (that is correct people, here on US soil), he's bowing to individuals from his own government.
- One of the most essential bows was the point at which he bowed to a Republican in 2010. One more city hall leader inside the USA, however somebody who was his lesser in the political arena.
- Again in 2012 at the G-20 highest point meeting, he is seen with the Obama handshake and make a beeline for the President of Mexico, Felipe Calderon.
- 2013, Obama bows to the President of Cuba, Raul Castro at the commemoration administration for the late President Nelson Mandela in South Africa.

In every one of these circumstances, Obama was reprimanded by individuals from the Associated Press and albeit right convention was explained consistently, it never entirely appeared to stick for past president Obama. Did he feel that it was a gesture of humility? Was it just his way of doing things on his own terms and showing that he was prepared to "stick it to the man?" We have no way of knowing what was going through his mind. What we cannot deny is that these were not by any means the only Presidential tactless act to be made during his time in the Oval Office (Ohlheiser, 2014)

PRISM

As a feature of the public authority's enemy of psychological oppression crusade following 9/11, the National Security Agency (NSA) has been given a decent lot of slack with regards to keeping an eye on people and having the option to assemble knowledge. One of these projects was sent off under the course of President Obama and was known as PRISM. This framework permitted the public authority to accumulate individual data from private residents assuming there was even the smidgen of association with gatherings or people that were associated with having connections to psychological oppressors. Crystal permitted the public authority to assemble individual information and data from organizations like Apple, Google, Microsoft and others, and despite the fact that it was carried out to balance psychological warfare on American soil,

increasingly more data is starting to become exposed with respect to this genuine danger to person's Fifth Amendment freedoms. The public authority is as yet being compelled to confess to keeping an eye on ordinary Americans as a component of their routine.

A whole 41-page slide show was spilled June 6, 2013 by both The Washington Post and The Guardian. The two media distributions affirm that PRISM is a top secret, exceptionally arranged program that empowers the FBI to acquire individual information from a rundown of locales that most Americans would utilize every day. A portion of these incorporate Google, Facebook, Yahoo, AOL, Microsoft, YouTube, Skype, as well as Apple.

When drawn closer by the Guardian and The Washington Post for input, not one of the above organizations professes to have any information on or interest in PRISM. As indicated by the records that had been released, both the FBI and NSA had direct admittance to every one of the servers having a place with these companies.

In light of the embarrassment, James Clapper, the US National Director of Intelligence minimizes these spilled reports and puts out a few announcements concerning the break according to the Intelligence point of view. He requests that the American public "believe that the organization regards common freedoms," an obscure explanation that probably won't rouse trust.

The next day, June 7, 2013, The Guardian dropped another bomb expressing that the UK has been engaged with PRISM beginning around 2010 working related to the NSA and has had the option to get to private messages from that point forward. President Obama affirms that it's occurring and that he knew about it for various years as of now. The main type of discourse that he's ready to go into is by remarking that "he's available to banter about it."

By June 9, 2013 the informant, Edward Snowden, approached asserting that he's answerable for the break. He additionally affirms that he's in Hong Kong and questions whether he will at any point see home once more. Following the call from the President that he would invite banter over the legitimacy of PRISM, pressure starts mounting for the public authority to declassify the program that has given the NSA and FBI unconditional power to keep an eye on Americans. Remembered for this is a solicitation that the program that permitted them to tap individuals' telephones likewise be disclosed. Inside the following ten days, the government delivers sufficient proof to help their cases that the program is as yet vital. The overseer of the NSA, General Keith Alexander affirms that there had been in excess of fifty psychological militant plots defeated right after 9/11 because of the program.

Understanding PRISM

This is a program that permits the people pulling the strings in states in the USA (and obviously the UK) to assemble individual information having a place with web clients and specialist organizations. It permits them to go through the entirety of your own messages and information to guarantee that you're not engaged with anything naughty or lined up with illegal intimidation. Evidently, PRISM started under the Bush organization and didn't have anything to do with President Obama, in spite of the fact that he plainly upholds keeping an eye on his own kin. A piece of PRISM is the Foreign Intelligence Surveillance Act (FISA) which appeared in 2006 and 2007 already.

What Makes PRISM Dangerous

The first spilled archive sent to The Washington Post and The Guardian ended up being real, rather than simply one more maniac after some significant fear inspired notion with expectations of acquiring some believability. The cases made by Snowden all ended up being genuine. Albeit each and every one of the online media and programming combinations referenced above have denied any information on or inclusion with PRISM, it appears to be hard to understand that these top specialist co-ops and pioneers in the innovation field would permit their information to be "hacked," particularly by the public authority, without their earlier information or endorsement. The PRISM calamity keeps on seething on. The public authority keeps on rejecting that they are keeping an eye on the American public, expressing rather that they scour through every one of these different stages looking for potential connects to psychological warfare or illegal intimidation plots.

Towards the finish of June 2013, Snowden figured out how to barely stay away from removal charges and getaway to Moscow with the assistance of Wikileaks. Here he is frantically looking for political asylum.

On June 29, 2013, a new arrangement of slides were spilled to the media. This time it's inferred that more than 100,000 dynamic targets are at present being reviewed. The new slides delivered end up being connected to constant dynamic checking of people by means of their messages, voice talks, and texts.

The American people group chose to voice their interests in regards to clear encroachments on three revisions. Those concerns connected with the primary correction, explicitly opportunity of get together, the fourth amendment connecting with search and seizure, and the fourteenth amendment which safeguarded residents with their overall freedoms to security inside their family, marriage, and homes. This alteration further connects with bringing up of youngsters. What PRISM had done was to encroach on every one of these natural privileges that were established on the rules that Americans would appreciate independence from persecution. This is actually the thing PRISM was starting to do.

The general population started denying the Kool-Aid the publiC authority was presenting that they were "just checking non-Americans" as a feature of the PRISM activity. The fact of the matter was that they were gathering two distinct sorts of data, content and metadata. The information that they're alluding to incorporates all happy of messages, VOIP, messages, messages, cloud reports, and different information documents. The second, metadata, would permit them to get close enough to different IP addresses. This would prompt a few different disclosures made by Snowden that ended up being authentic (T.C. Scottek, 2013).

Abuse of Executive Power

There have been multiple ways that the Obama Administration demonstrated to have abused the American Constitution more than some other Presidency in the White House. From working with a total negligence for the constitution, it's accounted for that he has gone out with the Constitution being more fragile than it was before his arrangement as 44th President of the United States (Rupp, 2016).

Had former President Obama set a precedent for the abuse of executive power in the White House? The style of Obama's decision-making process and not playing according to acceptable rules within the walls of government had set a dangerous precedent for the incoming President, Trump, to follow.

According to the New York Times, "Obama's quest for chief power without statement of regret... will shape the administration into the indefinite future." The Times would additionally portray "President Obama's two terms have been described by 'regulatory demolishing,' rather than official straightforwardness" (Binyamin Applebaum and Michael D, Shear, 2016).

Keystone XL Pipeline

Nobody could quite understand the reasons behind President Obama's flip flopping between his final decision not to approve the Keystone XL Pipeline that would carry crude oil from the oil sands regions in Alberta in Canada all the way to Nebraska. TransCanada would be liable for building the pipeline that had the ability to move 830,000 barrels of raw petroleum to the US day by day., It gave the idea that the pipeline would get the go-ahead from President Obama at first. It held the guarantee of occupation creation (Shapiro, 2017).

Concerns were raised in regards to ecological issues that could undermine the planet assuming the pipeline project went on. Outrageous natural activists started picketing at the White House. They called President Obama out on his choice to proceed with this undertaking. Whenever it was turning out to be obvious to TransCanada that Obama might pull out from the arrangement, they beseeched him to postpone his choice until after the 2016 races. Not having any desire to take a risk on the approaching organization, Obama killed the arrangement refering to that the pipeline would do essentially nothing to create extra work. It would barely influence the cost of unrefined petroleum [which had experienced a plunge at the time], and it undermined the climate. A portion of his crowd in this choice idea that Obama needed to be believed to be a natural draining heart.

Earlier we talked about "misleading banners" and this is by and large what occurred in the Keystone XL Pipeline bargain. While TransCanada was haggling with the public authority on Keystone, a lot of other pipeline bargains were being arranged and pushing ahead. Cornerstone might have been dismissed by Obama, yet this didn't impede further pipeline bargains from being finished up (Plumer, 2015).

Chapter 7: QAnon

"As a student of history, I have one or two doubts about paranoid fears in light of the fact that the world is unreasonably confounded to be overseen by a couple of extremely rich people drinking scotch behind a few shut entryways. But I do think that the voters are correct in sensing that they're really losing power. Also in response they give the framework a furious kick"

~ Yuval Noah Harari

Someone with the handle of "Unknown" starts posting obscure messages on talk sheets that are intended for significant PC people, 4chan. These messages initially begin showing up just after the Podesta email holes and begin alluding to the Pizzagate outrage. On these sheets there are either pictures or obscure pieces of information that are left. Each time, they appear to ensnare Hillary Clinton, the Cabal, and the underground government that is clearly running America. Messages infer that this underground government and secrecy are malicious and blames them for the absolute most intolerable wrongdoings. A portion of these violations incorporate dealing of youngster sex rings, sinister ceremonies, and even blames individuals for this mysterious society of being savages.

Mysterious cases that they have "Q" level freedom, which is a particular leeway level that is joined to the Department of Energy. They in this way approach some ordered data. Whoever "Mysterious" is, they give off an impression of being on Donald Trump and guarantee that he's the one in particular who can save America. Whenever Anonymous originally showed up on 4chan, there was theory that this was simply the President that was posting this load of stuff on the web. One reason for this is on the grounds that whoever this individual was, or alternately is, they are incredibly partial to President Trump and demonstrated that he is the main individual who can dispose of the abhorrent people inside the actual heart of the American government to "Make America Great Again."

4Chan

Once things started to get a piece warmed on 4chan, the arbitrators started trying
to close this individual or gathering of people down, and Anonymous moved over to 8chan. Mysterious cases that the messages are not really encoded, however frequently posts pictures or monograms for people. One of the previous posts demonstrated that Hillary Clinton was going to be captured by the FBI in regards to the server outrage and the 30,000 records. The date and opportunity arrived and went with no capture occurring. In every one of the messages that started being posted all the more often, they were just marked utilizing the underlying "Q", henceforth the name QAnon.

8Chan

8Chan was reaching the place where it could never again work under tension as things on the site started getting very dim and grisly. The proprietor of 8chan concluded that they at this point not needed anything to do with it and offered the site to a German person. The site changed its name to 8kun, and it was a complete wide open. Anybody who needed to post whatever there might do as such unafraid of control. It was this site that the FBI would ultimately target and power to close after a portion of the extreme postings of

QAnon.

It created the impression that while QAnon was supportive of Trump, they were likewise out to make an obvious argument against those individuals from the Cabal. They suggested that they had obtained specific noticeable structures in the USA where whenever spread out on a network guide and lines were drawn between other huge structures, they could demonstrate that this mysterious asAlong these linesciation was Satanic. Pictures can be observed where pentagrams interface these structures and by drawing pentagrams inside pentagrams it would prompt a structure with a 666 location. It was accepted that a portion of the organizations working out of this building were liable for concocting "ID chips" to be embedded in the wrist or on the temple of people for the purpose of distinguishing proof. This would likewise affirm predictions in the book of Revelations in the New Testament of the Bible, of "the stain of apostasy." QAnon further suggested that there were a lot more vile things occurring here. Shockingly, one of the proprietors of this building is the child in-law of President Donald Trump. So, we're not exactly certain how every one of that works out or squeezes into this equation.

Other central participants in this building incorporate Lucent Technologies, which QAnon recognizes similar to a Satanist association where the name is gotten from the word Lucifer. Meanwhile there's not the slightest bit of proof to demonstrate that any of this is verifiable. This is the thing QAnon's Q-Drops have been spreading. Normally any individual who is on the extreme right will lap all of this up as being totally factual.

What we want to explain here is that there are associations that are engaged with a few genuinely obscure dealings. In this way, it doesn't resist placing your head in the sand and imagining that these people are not out there. They are.

What all the data being unloaded on the web by QAnon ought to do is to make you mindful that evil unquestionably exists on the planet. Does it mean that you need to grab your rifle and go and shoot up an establishment? Absolutely not! No form of radical behavior should be tolerated. Apparently one of the sole motivations behind QAnon is to undermine the current government, in many examples causing inescapable panic.

Child Sex-Trafficking

Sex-dealing rings in all actuality do exist today that presently can't seem to be found. To affirm that they exist, you should simply take a gander at what Jeffrey Epstein and his sidekick Ghislaine Maxwell were getting up to while showing the US Government the center finger. Their activity proceeded unrestrained for a really long time and who can say for sure the number of lives were annihilated because of their conduct. No one knows what that "body count" of little youngsters was. What we can be sure of is that they were both associated with a few genuinely powerful people from legislators to lawyers. You don't turn into a very rich person with many individuals owing you leans toward coincidentally. You give a bit and reclaim a ton. No one knows the genuine story behind the thing these two were doing on Little St. James island, other than Ms. Maxwell.

Why should she implicate herself further when the only person who would really be able to implicate her 100 percent is dead? Do you see why questions upon questions begin to pile up as to whether Jeffrey Epstein did commit suicide or whether he was murdered? His prison term was served in luxury. What might be so unique this time? For what reason would he say he was so terrified to be

imprisoned? Was this is on the grounds that there was more proof against him this time rather than only a sales charge?

When he was let out of his past prison term, he went straight back to doing how he had forever been doing this multitude of little kids. What might make this encounter any unique? He was an incredibly well off man and would unquestionably have the option to pay right out of practically any circumstance that he found himself in.

We realize that he was being taped during private discussions among him and his lawyer. Did he offer something in this gathering that could implicate him much further in the sex-dealing charges? Was it his dark book with all his strong associations that got him killed?

Q as a Collective

Getting back to QAnon. We will allude to them as a group from now onwards on the grounds that albeit the first "Q" may have started innocuously as a solitary person. Right now, it is such a great deal greater than any one person. It has turned into a development of incredible magnitude and one

that is making the FBI very apprehensive. There have been countless records shut on sites, 4chan is down, 8chan/8kun is down, Facebook shut several thousand records, Twitter shut accounts, Reddit shut accounts. Every one of them attempted to conform to the FBI's declaration that QAnon is risky and comes close to illegal intimidation. Somehow or another assuming these super conservative people resort to viciousness and additionally hostility in any structure at all then the FBI are very right, devotees of QAnon can become risky (Ross, 2020).

Q-Drops

If they happen to simply be favorable to Trump allies or people who are only keen on fear inspired notions, then, at that point, there's no damage in after a portion of these breadcrumbs.

Shortly after Q-Drops started showing up more every now and again on the picture sheets, they started to acquire and more adherents as well as foothold inside the local area. In one of the conventions held by President Trump paving the way to the approaching political race later in 2020, QAnon devotees out of nowhere started showing up and fighting for the benefit of Trump. Out of nowhere it started to be extremely popular with different memorabilia, banners, identifications and patches being planned and offered to the developing allies of Q.

Anti-Elite

One of the principle points of QAnon is that they address all that is hostile to elitist. There have been derivations made that there will be an endeavored overthrow made by Obama, Hillary Clinton, and George Soros, the affluent extremely rich person to remove Trump. Until now, not at all like this has occurred, yet the allies of QAnon are turning out to be more extremist and more vocal with regards to taking care of business should this occur. They all appear to concur and be against the people who have the cash as well as the power, particularly in the event that they are not utilizing what they have astutely. How George Soros figured out how to certainly stand out enough to be noticed of QAnon is through the structure with the 666 location. It turns out that Soros either

claims the structure or put the cash up for the acquisition of the structure. He likewise has a few firms working out of a similar structure and was answerable for Lucent Technologies moving their base camp into a similar location. For Q devotees, this normally shouts pedophilic secrecy sweetheart and one world class that should be managed similarly as much as Obama and the Clintons.

Who is Q?

Although right toward the start of the absolute first "Drops," it created the impression that this was a solitary individual, it's presently accepted that there are a gathering of people who are Q. Rather than giving a great deal of important ordered data by serving it up on a plate, Q would prefer to give a few obscure subtleties that can be deciphered in different various ways. The thought is for the person to look for reality themselves. Like that, assuming Q were to at any point be recognized, they would have the option to guarantee, "conceivable deniability." Maybe what makes the whole Q peculiarity so enamoring is that there is a demeanor of secret around who this individual is and regardless of whether what they are driving you to is just down a dark hole, or towards tracking down reality (ADL, n.d.).

There have been other people who have confessed to setting up destinations and claiming to be Q. one of these destinations was begun and run by a security expert in New Jersey, Jason Gelinas. It's accepted that he was answerable for setting up the QMap site, yet chose to close it down in a matter of seconds afterwards.

Collusion with Trump?

Many have expected that since Q is so favorable to Trump that there is intrigue occurring between the individual(s) who are acting like Q and the President of the US. This hypothesis has been set by numerous resistance applicants and as per insights at present being accounted for, the quick development of QAnon allies is in direct extent to those extreme right fanatics who are as of now stirring up disdain and hostility. These people are moving back towards anti-Jewish practices, and this is what extremist faith in these fear inspired notions might actually do to somebody. What doesn't seem OK in the present circumstance is that the individuals who are generally that extreme right are against government, and insurrectionary which isn't going on here. This multitude of people are favorable to Trump.

What they are all against is the "underground government" that Trump continues to allude to, which is evidently the individuals who are truly running America. Remembered for this would be associations like the Illuminati, the Freemasons, and the Bilderberg Group. One isn't excessively sure which of them should call the shots as the Satanic religion of parasitic pedophiles? Whoever the "underground government" should be are the ones that the extreme right development are against (Sanburn, 2016).

Sole purpose of QAnon?

The sole motivation behind QAnon started as a blameless enough "drop board" on the profound web that was simply available to those PC nerds who knew where to look and how to scour the dim web. Not a lot of individuals see how 4chan, 8chan, or 8kun even worked. Certainly, there you could post text or pictures that were sufficiently obscure, or perhaps not even mysterious similarly as with a considerable lot of the previous posts or Q-Drops made on these destinations. At whatever point somebody could want lucidity, they could be replied with "Burrow Deeper" or "Follow the Breadcrumbs" - for the people who comprehended the wording, following the breadcrumbs was simply advising the peruser to keep following the strings, or revisiting strings that had effectively been posted.

Is QAnon a method for weakening the United States now? Who can say for sure? This is the thing they are being blamed for by the FBI. Are they intent on providing a misinformation overload on conspiracy theories that date back throughout most of our history? What is the end game of Q? It appears there are few people who are asking the right questions, yet a ton of paranoid fears are being tossed in with the general mish-mash to concoct far a larger number of inquiries than responds to (Francescani, 2020).

"Five Eyes"

Five Eyes is anything but another idea. Numerous people are just learning about them now since there have been references made by Q regarding the Five Eyes. They are alluded to as (FVEY). This knowledge collusion comprises of five English talking nations (or for the most part English-talking nations). These five nations are Australia, Canada, New Zealand, United Kingdom, and the United States of America. They have a place with a multilateral UKUSA arrangement (Canada, Australia, and New Zealand are as yet British Colonies) and there is a settlement set up for cooperation.

The Five Eyes deal was endorsed toward the finish of World War II. Everything revolves around data dividing among every one of the gatherings. Similar as Obama's PRISM program, to attempt to get Five Eyes, envision PRISM on steroids for every one of the nations addressed by the five countries included. Despite the fact that it is probably the most established deal in presence following World War II, it is at present under danger of significant breakdown, not from outside obstruction or dangers by different countries. All things being equal, the dangers are genuine and are coming from inside the Five Eyes nations themselves (Kim and Perlin, 2019).

The two primary explanations behind this long-standing collusion being under danger is on the grounds that arranged data has been spilled to the Russians, and there are main issues from the USA in regards to 5G innovation and the inclusion of Huawei, the Chinese innovation company.

The worry with 5G innovation is that it will have the ability to screen everything through your gadgets that it's a genuine danger to public safety. The USA Huawei war has been seething on for a few years at this point and they seem to in any case be at a stalemate. Canada seems to have comparable considerations and opinions on the Huawei front, while the UK appears to be very glad for Huawei to keep pushing ahead with these organizations. As per the Trump Administration, if this somehow happened to proceed, they might be compelled to reevaluate the data sharing settlement. America has consented to defer an official choice with regards to this issue until after the overall political decision towards the finish of 2020.

Chapter 8: Sex, Drugs, And Rock And Roll

"It is, I think, an unquestionable reality that Americans are, as Americans, the most hesitant individuals on the planet, and the most dependent on the conviction that different countries of the earth are in a trick to underestimate them"

~ Henry James

There are so many paranoid fears that continually encompass the people who have made it in Hollywood. A portion of these are totally peculiar, as "Stevie Wonder isn't exactly visually impaired," to, "the King (of Rock 'n Roll), Elvis Presley isn't dead, he's working for the FBI as a secret employable." What began this multitude of paranoid notions in any case? A portion of the most noteworthy volumes of mainstream society paranoid ideas concern the death of President John F. Kennedy. Since the time the mid sixties, paranoid ideas started to take structure and gratitude to extremist changes in innovation, these speculations have been filled and amplified..

There are hypotheses encompassing whether film chiefs coordinated explicit motion pictures that had their names connected to them, or regardless of whether they were simply nonentities and names to drive up deals inside films. Different speculations are that Emily Brontë didn't really compose Wuthering Heights since it was so "physically express" that no "woman" of the time would know about things like this. It was inferred that her sibling was the genuine writer of this renowned work of fiction.

We've as of now covered the "Who killed Natalie Wood" outrage as well as that of Marilyn Monroe. These two film symbols appear to have ruled the paranoid idea area for a really long time. It would astound you to discover that they're by all account not the only big name passings that have been tormented to death by questions.

Let's do a profound jump into a portion of these paranoid ideas that encompass the famous people within recent memory, as well as a portion of those from the past.

Blowin in the Wind - Bob Dylan

One such allegation is that The hit "Blowin in the Wind" sung by Bob Dylan was composed by a secondary school understudy in New Jersey. How did this talk begin? Essentially a secondary school understudy, Lorre Wyatt ends up tracking down the printed music for "Blowin in the Wind" in 1962 and makes it look like his own. It's accounted for in the secondary school's local area paper that Wyatt had composed the melody and this report is distributed a year prior to Dylan delivers his collection. The tune gets utilized in a band execution at the New Jersey secondary school, and on the grounds that the understudy had as of now asserted that the work was his own, it's thought to be valid. It's just in 1974 that Wyatt in the end concedes that he tracked down the printed music. There had effectively been a great deal of harm done to Dylan's standing. Let that be an example for all you lyricists out there. Continuously name your sheet music!

Shakespeare

There have been consistent hypotheses regarding Shakespeare. Many have contended that Shakespeare never truly existed on the grounds that it would be humanly difficult to compose such countless books and plays at that point. It's been theorized that a portion of these creators have been Sir Francis Bacon and Christopher Marlowe. The primary contention was that Shakespeare didn't have the insight to have composed the original copies as guaranteed. Marlowe should have passed on in 1593, which was then ventured to have been faked. Fanatics of his work accept that he composed under Shakespeare's name for the following 21 years.

The Mysterious Beatles

Speaking of odd, one hypothesis guarantees that the Beatles won't ever exist. I surmise that Along these linesmeone ought to have let Mark David Chapman know that before he killed John Lennon! There have additionally been claims related with the Beatles that Paul McCartney is dead and has been supplanted by a clone. So, we're not exactly certain who's been delivering all the music under Paul McCartney's name since the Beatles split up. Most of these theories started because people never believed that it was humanly possible for four young boys from Liverpool to be able to stick to the hectic schedule that was demanded of them as they became more and more famous. Well, then the same question should have been raised for other groups like the Rolling Stones and Queen.

Avril Lavigne 2.0

Another clone substitution that is being promoted as being valid is that of Avril Lavigne who clearly committed suicide in 2003. This fear inspired notion starts when Avril Lavigne recruits a clone, Melissa Vandella, to dump the paparazzi. Her fans accept that when she committed suicide in 2003, her record name wasn't ready to lose the cash they were making on her thus Melissa Vandella became Avril Lavigne 2.0. The way to demonstrating this whole paranoid idea is on the grounds that any individual who might sing "Sk8ter boi" could never wed somebody from Nickelback.

Stevie Wonder Can See

Getting back to Stevie Wonder, this hypothesis is considerably more silly. It's completely founded on the way that he is into ball and consistently demands courtside seats. The second piece of the hypothesis is apparently a photo that shows him snapping a picture of a wax sculpture of Michael Jackson and getting a mike stand mid-air.

Michael and Latoya Jackson Are the Same Person

Another totally mind boggling hypothesis is that Michael and Latoya Jackson were a similar individual. We're not quite sure how they managed to get past all the group photographs or pictures where the two are together? Maybe someone has answers to potential trick photography that may have been used? Does this mean that Michael Jackson is still alive?

Beyoncé's Baby

Specialist intrigue nuts accept that Beyoncé isn't exactly Blue Ivy's mother however is really Solange's all things being equal. How all of this began was with the way that Beyoncé appeared to be confounded with regards to her own due date when Blue Ivy was conceived. There's additionally an inconsistency in birth dates as indicated by when she was enlisted thus a ton of fans are asking why the mystery and change of birth dates Most scholars demand that Blue Ivy is really a substitute. The jury is as yet out on this one on the grounds that Beyoncé herself appears to be somewhat shocked and befuddled. Just to put any misinformation to rest with respect to Solange, assuming that Beyoncé was really her mom, she would have needed to have been conceived seven years sooner than what her real birth declaration says. Obviously, this hypothesis comes from somebody who professes to have heard the story through one more individual from the Knowles family!

Britney Spears Doesn't Sing All Her Own Songs

So, this hypothesis is probably evident. One of Britney Spears reinforcement vocalists sang somewhere around one of the melodies on her collections. The reinforcement vocalist, Myah Marie, has been singing with Britney for a couple of collections as of now. Hypothesis is that there are a few tunes where Marie is singing lead vocals rather than Britney. Marie's dad had spoken with Star magazine and affirmed over a year prior to the collection Britney Jean was delivered that his girl had the option to sound precisely like the popstar. There are assumed unpretentious contrasts between the manner in which a portion of the tunes on a similar collection sound. He lets the magazine know that in 2011, the studio addressing Spears paid Marie to sing seven of the twelve tracks on the collection. It just so happens, when Myah Marie is examined concerning this, she rejects that these charges have any legitimacy whatsoever.

Elvis

The intrigue encompassing the phony demise claims connecting with Elvis Presley were all complex. The initially was his solicitation to meet President Nixon in the White House. Normally, the President consented to this and there's a photo of Elvis and Nixon remaining on the White House steps. The subsequent case is somewhat more dependable. As per Ginger Alden, Elvis' life partner at the hour of his "passing" asserted that she had observed him lying on one of the bathroom floors at Graceland. As per the coroner, the reason for his demise was cardiovascular arrhythmia. For any individual who has a ton of familiarity with life systems or clinical phrasing, a cardiovascular arrhythmia is an unpredictable heartbeat. This implies that the patient is alive. Regardless of whether the coroner intended to specify something different on the demise authentication no one knows, however this has furnished all the Elvis trick scholars with something to bite on.

Bruce Lee

There are numerous scholars who find it difficult to accept that a pain reliever had the option to be the passing of one of the world's best and fittest people. As history would have it, Lee would bring a pain relieving and rests to sleep just to at absolutely no point awaken in the future. As indicated by the coroners' report, he experienced an unfavorably susceptible response to the pain relieving compound and this caused enlarging on the mind. Scheme scholars have attempted to observe different purposes behind his demise from either the Chinese Mafia or being hit by a deadly blow that could cause passing inside the space of days or weeks following the underlying blow. Bruce Lee was just 32 years old.

Brandon Lee

Son of the popular karate legend Bruce Lee, in one more disastrous occasion, Brandon Lee is shot while on set, shooting The Crow. Clearly, a prop weapon had been stacked with genuine ammo when it ought to have been holding spaces. By and by, his demise is connected to the Chinese Mafia similarly as with his renowned dad. The 28-year-old was going to send off his greatest film in his vocation to date, much similarly as Bruce.

Paul Walker

Following Typhoon Haiyan, Philippines, Paul Walker set up a cause to help casualties of this regular disaster.His noble cause, Reach Out Worldwide, was shaped in 2010 as a stage to help nations balancing out after catastrophic events. It's accepted by scholars that he picked some unacceptable cause to help with Typhoon Haiyan. Regardless of whether there was tax evasion included or a mystery plot to clean Philippinos, there were talks that the brakes of the Porsche Carrera GT that he was a traveler in at the hour of his passing had been altered. Nothing could be demonstrated with respect to these cases or allegations anyway as the whole vehicle had disintegrated and no proof of any sort stayed that could give indisputable evidence of tampering.

Cobain Was Murdered

Another paranoid notion that has been around always encompasses the passing of Kurt Cobain in 1994. Nirvana fans have been guessing that he was killed by Courtney Love for a really long time. A month prior to he was observed shot in the head, Cobain was hospitalized evidently for taking an excessive number of analgesics. Love would later affirm that the explanation Cobain took so many pain relievers in Rome was for his fans to acknowledge his self destruction in Seattle. She illustrates how discouraged he was and the way in which he needed to end it all.

A private examiner into Cobain's demise would give some chilling proof that brought up a larger number of issues than gave replies. He affirms that there were no fingerprints on the gun that killed Cobain. The coroner found he had multiple times the deadly portion of heroin in his framework. This would have delivered him oblivious, not to mention permitting him to place the firearm in his mouth and pulling the trigger. His medication unit was additionally tidied up and taken care of, which would have been something he could not have possibly had the option to do had he taken narcotics found in his bloodstream.

Moon Landing Hoax

Okay so this fear inspired notion doesn't fall very inside the sex, medications, and rowdy 'equation, however it falls under cinematography. Numerous connivance scholars accept that the whole moon landing was a fabrication and was shot at Area 51. It's accepted that Stanley Kubrick, the popular film chief was

associated with this "phony" moon landing and that Kubrick really goes on record conceding so a lot. The justification for faking the moon arrival to beat the Russians to the moon obviously. For what reason do as such numerous Americans actually put stock in this paranoid idea after different researchers have approached from MIT expressing that the moon arrival was genuine?

For this hypothesis to be confirmed, as in, Apollo truly arrived on the moon, various inquiries have been raised concerning why it's never been rehashed by some other superpower since then.

Considering innovation of the day, particularly when it came to PCs, it isn't accepted by scholars that there was the limit with respect to on-board PC frameworks to work sophistically enough inside such a little space as the lunar module. At the point when PCs initially surprised the world, most servers were set up in huge rooms, interlinked with each other. Would NASA be able to have truly developed this state of the art innovation before IBM and other driving PC specialists? Assuming this is the case, for what reason were these miniature PCs not imparted to the world?

Not just that, however no other person has at any point endeavored to arrive on the moon. Certainly someone would be keen on catching the USA banner that is up there. 2019 saw a bombed endeavor by the Italians at arriving at the moon and this is roughly a long time since the main guessed moon landing occurred. What evidence do people have that Stanley Kubrick coordinated the "phony moon landing?" People have highlighted different motion pictures that he has coordinated 2001*: A Space Odyssey where there are various similitudes between the thing was broadcast similar to the moon arrival in 1969.*

The subsequent inquiry presented is who was recording Apollo 11 at that point? Once more everything appears to be perfectly wrapped up with a bow, yet after looking into it further there are a larger number of inquiries than addresses. Even the Russians, who were successful in orbiting the Earth numerous times a few years after the supposed moon landing never actually made it to the moon.

Another inquiry that is never been replied by anybody at NASA or Anywayme other establishment in regards to the trip to the moon is that all pictures sent back to the Earth show simply the Earth with a totally dark foundation. So, what has befallen every one of the stars? Certainly from space you're ready to see a portion of these divine phenomena.

Who Killed Diana

One of the biggest fear inspired notions that are as yet out there today encompass the demise of the Diana Princess of Wales, otherwise called the People's Princess. The Princess was killed during a rapid mishap including the Mercedes Benz she was going in. The vehicle collided with a support point in the Alma span in Paris not long after 12 PM. Dodi Fayed, 41-year-former beau of Diana's, Henri Paul, the driver of the vehicle, and Diana are totally killed during the accident. Trevor Rees-Jones, Diana's guardian, is the main one to endure the accident.

Investigations into the mishap by both British and French authorities infer that the mishap was brought about by Henri Paul who had driven the vehicle while affected by liquor. It additionally makes notice that he because driving so quick was to lose the paparazzi that had been after the couple the entire day. The scenery of the story was that the couple had gone through the day sunbathing on Dodi Fayed's yacht. Bothered by the paparazzi the entire day. They weren't even ready to shake the media following a supper at the upmarket Ritz lodging in Paris. The couple left through a back access to the lodging to lose the media. This was ineffective and brought about the press pursuing them in vehicles, and on bikes. It's accepted that this would at last prompt their deaths.

Conspiracy speculations have reliably encircled this mishap since the time this occurred in 1997. There have been requests and speculations into the mishap. From hints that she was pregnant, and her family were miserable regarding her relationship with the Egyptian mogul. Different hypotheses were that MI6 were some way or another associated with her demise. The purposes behind associations with MI6 is because of a previous specialist, Richard Tomlinson who was excused for releasing delicate material. Tomlinson inferred that Diana and Dodi's demise resemble plans that MI6 needed to kill the President of Serbia in 1992. Albeit this was explored, Tomlinson's cases were ultimately excused as manufacture. The justification for why MI6 would have at any point been involved would have been under express guidelines of the Duke of Edinburgh, Prince Phillip. Dodi Fayed's dad kept on faulting MI6 for the passings all through the examination (Telegraph Reporters, 2017).

Were there motivations behind why the Royal Family might have had any desire for her dead? Totally. There were tales that Diana knew an excessive number of things that might have brought the Royal Family into notoriety. It was accepted that Diana was perhaps mindful of an assault episode that had occurred at Buckingham Palace. A large number of her nearby partners demanded that she was going to totally expose things happening straightforwardly under the Queen's nose. Whether or not this was valid must be theorized in light of the fact that she never lived to tell the tale.

Further to an examination into their demises that were just finished in April 2008, it was reasoned that the paparazzi who had sought after their vehicle, as well as their driver, Henri Paul were answerable for gross carelessness and were to be faulted for the passings of Diana and Dodi on this decisive evening. It had required sixteen years for the jury to arrive at this resolution, as well as expressing that the couple might have endure the lethal mishap assuming they had been wearing their safety belts (Nicolaou, 2019).

Chapter 9: LA LA Land

"In a culture filled by burnout, a culture that has run itself down, our public versatility becomes compromised. Also when our aggregate resistant framework is debilitated, we become more powerless to infections that are essential for each culture since they're important for human instinct - manipulation through scare tactics, scapegoating, paranoid ideas, and demagoguery"

~ Arianna Huffington

According to Brian Friedenberg much of what's currently taking place in the US has very similar undertones to some deep, dark anti-Semitic beliefs and behaviors that date back decades. He sees the data that QAnon is spilling on the web as being demonstrative of the dull web again. The paranoid idea of QAnon is fit as a fiddle in Hollywood and it's causing a taking care of free for all among A-listers all through Los Angeles.

Oprah Winfrey

Kat Tenberge from Insider (2o2o) covers a considerably more peculiar story that breaks in Hollywood toward the start of 2020 asserting that Oprah Winfrey was captured by police in Boca Raton. She was blamed for running one of the youngster sex-dealing rings. As a component of a nature, Oprah conveys a tweet exposing the case and tells everybody that she's socially removing like every other person in America at that point. This does essentially nothing to quietness the taking care of free for all of QAnon extreme right allies who keep getting the message out that Oprah had been "struck" and was presently making a beeline for jail. Not even affirmation from the Boca Raton police office does a lot to drench the flares that were consuming poor Oprah at the stake.

What carried Oprah into the focus of QAnon's degree in the principal occurrence were claims that "Top notch famous people were associated with these youngster sex-dealing rings." Did that put a programmed focus on the rear of each of the "Elite VIPs?" According to online media expert, Michael Coudrey, who breaks down and exposes counterfeit news via web-based media routinely, cautions that in most cases these sorts of paranoid notions are ended up being false. What is by all accounts adding foothold to QAnon and every one of the hypotheses being tossed into the electronic local area, alongside people being isolated and house-bound, there will undoubtedly be development in the conservative development. He affirms that which got going as something of an innocuous trick, the American populace appear to be truly affected by these stories.

Many of the QAnon versus Oprah hypotheses began on Facebook rather than any of different channels. When there, the tales started to fan out like quickly as they went totally popular via online media. As a result of COVID-19 there were a larger number of individuals savaging the web than typical. Reddit reports that they're encountering a significant spike in rush hour gridlock. Coronavirus is in a real sense putting the whole world behind their screens and this implies that QAnon has an engaged crowd. A group of people that is ready to acknowledge anything they're being taken care of, even the smallest of "breadcrumbs" (Tenbarge, 2020).

Who Are the Major Players?

According to QAnon, those that have as of now been distinguished before as pedophiles are engaged with this evil cabal.

Bill Cosby

He was expressed as being associated with these sex-dealing rings. After all he's right now spending time in jail in the Phoenix State Correctional Institution. The charges-brutal sexual stalker. Toward the start of the primary influx of COVID-19 to hit the US, there were a couple of old detainees who were moved to keep them from getting this lethal sickness. In spite of the fact that NBC reports that there are a few detainees moved under extraordinary request, Cosby isn't one of them. We're not exactly specific how 82-year-old visually impaired Bill Cosby actually squeezes into the QAnon story, yet the writing is on the wall. His past crimes have caught up with him and even once released, he will be labelled as a sexual predator that's a danger to society.

Clare Bronfman – NXIVM

Before we can perceive you who Clare Bronfman is, we really want to turn around and give you somewhat more data on the NXIVM sex faction. This clique was shaped on the rear of a staggered fraudulent business model. Its vital targets to people in general at large was self-awareness and tracking down your direction to illumination. Numerous people saw Keith Raniere, the prime supporter of the religion, as a master. This religion of sex slaves had been happening since the 1990s. Ladies were enrolled from varying backgrounds, various foundations and various ages. They should have been arranged to offer a few things to enter this "restrictive sorority" of sex slaves. The initially was offering individual proof that could be utilized to implicate them or coerce them would it be a good idea for them they at any point wish to leave the gathering. This was regularly through compromising video film or compromising photos. These were completely kept by Raniere to extort these ladies in the event that they at any point attempted to leave the association (Press, 2020).

Clare Bronfman, an advocate of the association for a long time, has recently been condemned to 81-months detainment for her part in the clique. She confessed to keeping an unlawful person who was being utilized for "work and administrations'' without installment. During the time she was associated with NXIVM, she had submitted Visa extortion, bankrolled the association with a huge number of dollars, and fit the bill for Raniere's safeguard in the charges that were brought against him. As per the Associated Press, she has proposed to repay $6 million, as well as a $500,000 fine (Li, 2020; Press, 2020).

Keith Raniere – NXIVM

He was originator and head of the sex-dealing ring referred to just as NXIVM. Conceding to all charges, he was answerable for coercing those inside his "group of concubines" of sex slaves. He'd by and by made them and marked them with his initials to keep them in line. The gathering assumed the type of a faction working out of Albany. The principal gathering of "sex slaves" had to request to be marked for the purpose of demonstrating their total dependability to Keith Raniere. He had been straightforwardly engaged with making the marking custom along with entertainer Allison Mack.

During this "conciliatory" process, the ladies or youngsters would should be totally bare. They would need to remain with a particular goal in mind with their legs spread separated, arms likewise being perhaps held down during the marking custom. Whenever marking had happened, these ladies were then alluded to as slaves. At the point when it was first delivered that there would be a request done into the sex-clique, Raniere gave his all to separate himself from it, expressing that while he was the fellow benefactor of the association he had no information on what was happening right in front of him (Kranc, 2020).

Some of the ones who figured out how to get away from this religion have transparently talked about what happened in secret and that Raniere had regularly engaged in sexual relations with underaged young ladies. As a component of the marking function, they were to allude to him as grandmaster from there on and they had a place with him. The first tier of women was then tasked with finding and training the next group of women and so on. Taking into account that this faction was first framed during the 1990s and was never checked, it's hard to envision precisely the number of ladies were engaged with this "collection of mistresses of sex-slaves" (Grigoriadis, 2018).

It's accounted for that there were significant measures of cash paid towards the gathering from in excess of 16,000 people. This cash should pay for "self improvement classes all through the US, Mexico, and Canada" (Moynihan, 2020). At the hour of composing this book, he is as yet anticipating sentencing!

Kevin Spacey

In 2018, Kevin Spacey posted a video on YouTube named "How about we be Frank." His main aim was to attempt to spread the news that individuals will struggle rebuffing him for the [approximately] thirty sexual wrongdoing counts that have been asserted at that point. The sole reason for the video is to occupy from the news occurring around him. There are similitudes to one of the person's he plays in House of Cards, Frank Underwood. In 2016 he's blamed for physically attacking an eighteen-year-old. The main charge to land toward Spacey was that of Anthony Rapp, who he is sorry to for his conduct. With respect to the next 29 charges, best to keep quiet. Spacey doesn't have anything to say (Kornhaber, 2018).

There have been a few reports of film sets being shut on the grounds that Spacey has made improper advances to youthful people. As indicated by Gabriel

Byrne, an all out examination concerning Spacey was directed by the "Place of Cards" group in 2012 and he was shipped off be retrained while the set is shut. Others who have approached have talked about outrageous post horrible disorder PTSD following Spacey grabbing them. One more affirmed that he was just fifteen years of age when 24-year-old Spacey endeavored to assault him. Probably the most concerning issue with assault is that the casualty is the person who feels disgraceful and meriting whatever happened to them. This is the means by which this individual portrayed his experience to Vulture magazine (Jung, 2017).

There was a positive association with Jeffrey Epstein and the flight logs that have quite recently been unlocked incorporate Spacey as a long standing customer. Presently flight logs that are being circled all around the web. This is following the capture of Ghislaine Maxwell toward the start of July 2020. All that these "spilled" flight logs are doing are making more extensive theory regarding which Hollywood A-listers could have had associations with Epstein. While a considerable lot of the names on the rundown are phony and have been exposed for what they are, there are likewise names that show up in his "little dark book." This dark book seems to hold the way to a large number of the things that Epstein and Maxwell were doing. The fundamental message here isn't to just acknowledge the primary "guarantee made through Twitter" or on "Facebook" similar to the essential reality of what is happening. A significant part of the data in regards to the Epstein sex ring has kicked the bucket with him and it's far fetched that Maxwell will ensnare herself in her forthcoming preliminary (Kornhaber, 2018; Kelly, 2020).

Harvey Weinstein

Between October 5, 2017 and May 29, 2020, I could never have delighted in being from Harvey Weinstein's perspective. Claims keep on moving in against the Hollywood head honcho extending back very nearly thirty years. Here is a short foundation of a portion of the names that openly opposed Weinstein and his "celebrated" film vocation (BBC Entertainment and Arts, 2019):

- Rose McGowan, Ashley Judd, Romola Garai (a British entertainer) blames him for mistakes when she was just eighteen years old.
- October 10, 2017 - Thirteen ladies approach in The New Yorker with three claims including assault. Weinstein denies everything. The same day Asia Agento claims that Weinstein constrained himself on her in the south of France in 1997. For Stoller, it's in 2004. Mira Sorvino who showed up in large numbers of his movies affirmed that he was continually constraining her to become engaged with an actual relationship. The next to come forward are none other than Angelina Jolie and Gwyneth Paltrow – both confirm they were harassed by him. As though his day could deteriorate, his significant other, Georgina Chapman declares that she's leaving.
- October 12, 2017 - Rose McGowan affirms through Twitter that she had been assaulted by Weinstein.
- October 13,2017 - A previous office associate blames Weinstein for attempting to draw her into one more space for a "massage."
- Kate Winslet, Lysette Anthony, Lauren Holly, Lena Headey, Lupita Nyong'o, Zelda Perkins, Brit Marling, Mimi Haleyi, Dominique Huett, Natasha Malthe, Annabella Sciorra, Daryl Hannah, Paz de la Huerta, Uma Thurman, Kadian Noble, Salma Hayak, thus the rundown of A-rundown entertainers go on. They come in a real sense slithering out of the woodwork to get Harvey Weinstein to pay for his crimes.
- It is just in March 2020 that he is at last sentenced for certain instances of assault and rape. He is condemned to 23 years in prison.
- No sooner is Weinstein condemned except for one more four ladies approach guaranteeing assault and sexual wrongdoing. One of these

ladies was seventeen at the hour of the incident.

In all the time from the three years between the underlying allegations becoming public and his condemning, Harvey Weinstein loses everything. He is compelled to leave, is deprived of his relationship with the Academy and he is criticized by the absolute greatest names inside the movie business (BBC Entertainment and Arts, 2019).

Anthony Weiner

Following the revelation of the private server that Hillary Clinton was utilizing preceding her 2016 political race. She is found possessing a PC that had a place with the spouse of her top guide, Huma Abedin, Anthony Weiner.

Weiner was blamed for sending express messages to a minor. The FBI liable for finding the messages accepts that the case wasn't managed accurately. The FBI specialist, John Robertson, sees that there's no development working on it and chooses to move toward the US Attorney's office straightforwardly. The reaction he got was to wipe all hint of his association with the case from his PC (Bates, 2020).

Robertson turns out to be much more disappointed and accepts that the FBI might need to point the fault toward him. A further 600,000 messages between Hillary Clinton and Abedin are found on Weiner's PC. You read the above figure correctly—emails between just two individuals amount to more than half a million communications yet they aren't on official or protected laptops. The greatest inquiry of all is the reason are Abedin's messages on Weiner's laptop?

Former Director of the FBI, James Comey opens and shuts the case rapidly giving Clinton and her staff the supposed "token punishment" for being reckless. Nonetheless, Comey resumed the examination towards the finish of October when it was uncovered that Weiner was sexting with a student. Weiner's PC is seized once more, and Robertson is answerable for going through it once more. He finds significantly more messages among Abedin and Clinton. By and by Comey shuts the examination. The book, October Surprise: How the FBI Tried to Save Itself and Crashed an Election, by Devlin Barrett uncovers that Robertson was at that point worried about the 600,000 messages in September as of now (before the case was reopened).

Robertson's options were limited in regards to the Abedin/Clinton messages on the grounds that the FBI summon was restricted in its extension and wouldn't permit Robertson admittance to these documents. Yet again in light of the obscene idea of what's on Weiner's PC, as well as what were obviously government archives, Robertson illuminates his bosses what he's found, and indeed nothing!

His principle concern was that a few pedophiles approached touchy government data and admittance to Hillary Clinton's records. Moving toward the investigators of the case, he let them know that he was terrified. In the report that Comey gave, he affirmed that there were just 30,000 messages. These figures as indicated by Robertson were absolutely fake. Once more as he continued to request that how manage the 600,000 messages between Hillary Clinton and Abedin he was in the long run quieted and told to scour his PC of all hints of the examination. One of the examiners asked him whether

he was ready to be an informant. Once he'd scrubbed his computer, he decided that it would be best to send himself a "Letter to Self" which he included "I have deep misgivings about the institutional response of the FBI to the congressional investigation into the Hillary Clinton email matter." In a similar email, he affirms that the whole matter appeared to be an instance of "CYA," or all in all, "cover your a**."

Comey at last concurs that a warrant might be important to research the Weiner PC and messages further. Time is drawing nearer towards the decisions and the case is returned and afterward reclosed only two days before the overall political race. President Trump concludes that the model that Comey set for approximately 35,000 FBI specialists in the managing of the messages on Anthony Weiner's PC is enough for him to be terminated (Bates, 2020).

Anthony Weiner concedes of sexting a minor and is condemned to 21 months in jail. He wound up just a brief time prior to being delivered before. The condition was that he register as a sex wrongdoer (Diebel, 2018).

Other Conspiracy Theories Gaining Traction

Amid every one of these mystery secrecy, savage sex-dealing pedophiles who are truly running the US (as per QAnon) there have been other paranoid ideas tossed in with the general mish-mash. We will think about each of these momentarily and indeed surrender them to you to conclude whether they legitimize your consideration or regardless of whether you can expose them on your own.

COVID-19 - #Plandemic

Another hypothesis that will not disappear is that the Coronavirus is a synthetic illness made by the proprietor of Microsoft, Bill Gates. A portion of the narratives connected to this are that the Coronavirus isn't deadly, it doesn't kill, and has been made by those trusting in genetic counseling or populace control. These people allude to the COVID-19 pandemic as a #Plandemic made to control individuals. They are persuaded that plans upheld to keep individuals inside have been executed by the mystery secrecy. A similar secrecy that's

battling for a New World Order (Spring and Wendling, 2020; Stanford, 2020).

You can find the #Plandemic supporters at rallies all over the world now and they're not just limited to the US. They refuse to avoid social distancing, wear face masks, or remain indoors. For them, all information regarding the COVID-19 narrative is being controlled by governments (the deep state government) as a means of scare tactics and mind control. Another age-old conspiracy theory of mind control, known as Project MK Ultra, that was run by the CIA is being linked to COVID-19.

Dr. Mikhail Varshavski, otherwise called Dr. Mike, is a confirmed General Practitioner who teaches patients on various clinical issues. He as of late ran a whole "Point-by-Point 'Plandemic' Smackdown" on a video that was becoming a web sensation. It was a meeting with Judy Mikovits and Mikki Willis, a producer who had created two separate narratives to demonstrate that Bill Gates as well as Dr. Anthony Fauci, top of the National Institute of Allergies and Infectious Disease NAID and his agent, Clifford Lane, as making the Coronavirus for the express reason for bringing in cash. Toward the start of this "smackdown," Dr. Mike affirms as a clinical specialist he can give remarks on clinical realities and data as it's introduced to him.

The video record has Judy Mikovits embroiling the two specialists Anthony Fauci and Clifford Lane as being liable for making both an illness and a fix which they have protected for the express motivations behind making money.

So, this is the place where Dr. Mike chooses to burrow somewhat more profound. As far as he might be concerned, it doesn't appear to be legit at all that these clinical specialists would gamble with their licenses for some immunization. He tracks down the responses to his inquiries in the British Medical Journal. It's affirmed that Dr. Fauci needed to add his name to the patent vault and as such was qualified for explicit remuneration yearly. Not concurring with this interaction, all assets got by Dr. Fauci are given to a foundation. At the point when it came to Dr. Path, the aggregate sum of pay he'd got since this antibody was enlisted in 1997 has been a sum of $45,000, barely a sum worth losing your clinical permit over.

Mikovits gives her consideration regarding Bill Gates and blames him for directing cash towards the innovative work of immunizations to fix the Covid. Dr. Mike checks her contention by guaranteeing that Bill Gates gives to numerous compassionate causes and this sounds simply one more one. Through his establishment, work had as of now concocted an antibody to treat the infection. What had been affirmed by the two was the way that the establishment wouldn't acknowledge any award or acknowledgment whether any of the immunizations were viewed as viable. The establishment would give the antibody to the whole world without enlisting it or licensing the equation. In the event that there was shortcoming found with this, the issue lay with Mikovits herself.

Dr. Mike proceeded to communicate his esteem for the numerous altruistic endeavors that Bill Gates and his establishment had effectively contributed towards over numerous years (Varshavski, 2020).

Vaccinations

Conspiracy hypotheses actually rage with respect to immunizations. This is another paranoid idea that isn't new. It appears to have endured for an extremely long period that

getting immunizations some way or another make you helpless or more defenseless to illness and can prompt other emotional wellness issues. This fear inspired notion can be broken into two separate sections:

Coronavirus Vaccine and Microchip Implants

This returns to some of what was exposed by Dr. Mike above. It is basically impossible that that Bill Gates is associated with both of these plans, other than research financing to track down an answer for treat flow COVID-19 strains of the Coronavirus. Both Bill Gates and his significant other Melinda who head up the Gates Foundation have exposed the hypothesis with the British Broadcasting Corporation (Spring and Wendling, 2020).

This all returns to remarks made by Bill Gates in March 2020 when he affirmed in a meeting "at last we will have a few advanced authentications which would be utilized to show who'd recuperated, been tried, and eventually who got an antibody." There had been no notice of central processor during any of these meetings. This and numerous other paranoid notions have encircled Bill Gates on the rear of his empathy and worry for humankind (Goodman and Carmichael, 2020).

5G

Recent National Pew Research (NPR) results show most Americans are persuaded that getting inoculations against COVID-19 was a reason. They accept that computer chips will be embedded in their arm or on their brow. Back to the book of Revelations and the "sign of evil". It's generally accepted that once the 5G organization is enacted the public authority would have the option to track and follow everything you might do. This has begun a monstrous enemy of 5G development. In the wake of talking in excess of twelve people the NPR reports how a portion of these speculations can become believable.

The key is having something possible. It shouldn't be valid, simply conceivable. For this hypothesis to be conceivable, computer chips are referenced as the planned guilty party. December 2019 saw a paper distributed by certain analysts from MIT in the diary, *Science Translational Medicine*. The

paper illustrated that it was feasible for "quantum spots" to be conveyed to the skin to record vaccinations.

One of the specialists on the undertaking at that point, Kevin McHugh, colleague teacher of bioengineering at Rice University is confused by the micro processor thought. He keeps any information from getting computer chips in his unique examination. He expresses that "all the quantum dabs do is produce light" (Evestatieva, 2020).

Conclusion

"While we might fault the web for the straightforwardness with which fear inspired notions multiply, the net is truly significantly more guilty for the manner in which it interfaces everything to nearly all the other things. The hypertext interface, as we used to call it, permits any reality or ide to turn out to be personally associated with any other"

~ Douglass Rushkoff

As we arrive at the finish of this work that is jam loaded with paranoid idea after fear inspired notion, you will see the way simple it is to become dependent on anything new story is being spread. Not all the data introduced here is unadulterated scheme. Quite a bit of it depends on truth with proof to validate and uphold claims. This is one of the keys while choosing for yourself whether something is only a paranoid notion set before you to explicitly lose you course. Are sure occasions revealed through the media misleading banners? It is positively getting to the age where you want to twofold check and triple check information.

Whether there is a genuine "dark state," an "evil cabal that is trafficking children as sex-workers" and even worse, none of our investigations have been able to provide conclusive proof and evidence to this happening. Other than the sex-dealing ring constrained by extremely rich person Jeffrey Epstein and his accomplice Ghislaine Maxwell, we are dubious concerning who different players might be in these disgusting abominations that were done on these youthful girls.

Will we at any point truly know the reality of these grievous violations against young ladies? It's far fetched, except if proof attends light in the court date of Ghislaine Maxwell or then again assuming that different observers get out of the shadows. Was Epstein quieted on account of his nearby associations with the Clintons? Who can say for sure? The fact that he really did makes there still no proof to demonstrate that him never ended it all similarly as there no proof. The accommodation of camera's going down right at that point, as well as watchmen not being outside his cell lead to considerably a greater number of inquiries than answers.

Other paranoid notions we realize we can cling to, despite the fact that they've been around since the occasions happened are whether the FBI or CIA were

really associated with President John F. Kennedy's death? Did MI6 have a say in the demise of Diana, Princess of Wales, and Dodi Fayed? Who concealed the homicides of Marilyn Monroe, Natalie Wood, and Curt Cobain? For every one of these alleged suicides, there were individuals working behind the scenes tidying up scenes and ensuring that main those things they needed were found.

Getting back to QAnon and the accompanying that they have figured out how to acquire north of a three-year time frame, it's not difficult to see the reason why it's feasible for individuals to put stock in a portion of the pernicious bits of hearsay they are spreading. All people have opportunity to data and opportunity to accept anything they desire to believe.

The Illuminati, the Freemasons, and Bilderberg are exceptionally cryptic associations. They generally have been. Does this imply that they're running mysterious youngster sex-dealing rings, or tormenting kids to deplete them of their blood for something known as an adrenochrome? This should be a type of sexual enhancer when consumed by grown-ups however is just found in kids. It's created by the youthful adrenal organs when a youngster turns out to be incredibly terrified. This is probably what these mystery secrecy, A-listers are later and why such countless kids have been recorded missing. The numbers as they presently stand are around 800,000 youngsters in the United States, 134,000 in the United Kingdom, and two or three 100,000 kids in Germany. These measurements are completely accumulated north of a year time frame (Friedenberg, 2020).

It turns out to be difficult to understand that assuming this were occurring, what might occur with every one of the youngsters a short time later? While these insights are incredibly high for every one of these nations, those working with various youngster promotion bunches are not all succumbing to these freshly discovered convictions that adrenochrome even exists.

> <u>As a sidebar:</u> In China, there has been something almost identical that was occurring to their "moon" bears. Their bile was being reaped as a feature of current home grown medication and it was guaranteed that this blend was additionally a Spanish fly. It has taken promotion bunches working intimately with different players, from clinical experts to the higher classes of government to intercede to safeguard these bears. The method involved with acquiring the bile from these bears was done under the most harsh circumstances imaginable.

Could this truly be going on to large numbers of the youngsters who have vanished? Is it possibly conceivable that this sexual enhancer exists and is accepted to be the best "high" that anybody might ever experience?

Let's consider briefly that penances were being made? We realize that there are houses of worship of Satan that have been set up all through the US. Does anyone have statistics of what their membership numbers are? How would you be able to join these "Orders" like the entrance fee that needed to be paid to join NXIVM? What takes place behind closed doors of all these secretive organizations will continue to fan the flames of conspiracy theory for many years to come.

As we consider Q, either as a single individual or as a collective? What is their endgame? What is it that they are trying to achieve? Is their sole purpose to disrupt the current elections that are about to take place in the US? QAnon has become much bigger than just the United States though. There are groups popping up all over the world that have clearly drank the Kool-Aid and believe in absolutely everything being fed to them. This is effectsly affecting families and connections.

Because of COVID-19 and lockdown systems, numerous people have had much additional free time than expected. This has permitted them to examine or follow a portion of the breadcrumbs left by Q, particularly for them to find. Q has forever been very unpretentious and there are numerous things anticipated by them that poor person work out as expected. For those strict proponents who are hanging on absolutely every word, gathering together to fuel one another up at rallies and urging others to "join the movement" stop and think for a moment whether there's a shred of evidence that does or ever has pointed to the truth?

As referenced over, perhaps the best gift to accompany the American Constitution is both right to speak freely and opportunity of conviction. Everybody is qualified for structure their own viewpoint prior to saying something regarding this. One of only a handful of exceptional things that I ask is that as you do, keep a receptive outlook. Consider everything that could have been created absolutely as a media hype?

If you have family or companions who have become tied up with deception or scheme, attempt and comprehend what they are used to without permitting something however disastrous as a large group of slanted fear inspired notions that seem to be so firmly woven together to destroy you or your loved ones. Try not to delay until it

is past the point of no return before you take care of somebody who looks like they're following that white bunny down the deep, dark hole. It will just fan a fire that may currently be seething. You need to have a relationship to return to.

If individuals are attempting to persuade you to commit to them following QAnon, recollect that you and just you have a decision to make. Up to this point, we have endeavored to give you however many realities and data as we can. These realities have been painstakingly explored to give you a lot greater picture and to see things from various points. You can choose for yourself. Is QAnon there to weaken the forthcoming political race process? Or then again, do they accept the things they're placing out on the web?

Conspiracy scholars can be perilous to both themselves and society at large. Pick carefully and settle on any choice having investigated current realities as intently as possible. Tragically, in light of the fact that the FBI marked QAnon a potential psychological oppressor danger, many posts have been erased. Different destinations presently return an "mistake code" demonstrating that the site's been taken out. Getting at reality could mean a ton of burrowing and research. My suggestion is that you be ready for what you could find. Cheerful chasing after those reality searchers out there.

References

ADL. (n.d.). *QAnon*. Against Defamation League. https://www.adl.org/qanon

Aguirre, H. (2019, July 20). *The abhorrences of Jeffrey Epstein's private island*. Vanity Fair; Vanity Fair. https://www.vanityfair.com/news/2019/07/abhorrences-of-jeffrey-epstein-private-island

Barkun, M. (2003). *A culture of intrigue: Apocalyptic dreams in contemporary America (first ed.)*. Berkeley University of California

Press.

Bates, D. (2020, September 18). *Hillary Clinton email informant recounts his frustration with FBI.* Mail Online. https://www.dailymail.co.uk/news/article-8748293/Hillary-Clinton-email-informant tells-disappointment FBI.html

BBC Entertainment & Arts. (2019, January 10). Harvey Weinstein course of events: How the scandal unfolded. *BBC News*. https://www.bbc.com/news/amusement expressions 41594672

BBC News US & Canada. (2016, October 27). *18 Revelations from Wikileaks' hacked Clinton messages.* BBC News. https://www.bbc.com/news/amp/world-us-canada-37639370

BBC News US & Canada. (2019, November 16). Jeffrey Epstein: The lender accused of sex dealing. *BBC News*. https://www.bbc.com/news/world-us-canada-48913377

Bekiempis, V. (2020, July 31). *Ghislaine Maxwell prepared underage young ladies as sex slaves, records assert.* The Guardian. https://www.theguardian.com/us-news/2020/jul/31/ghislaine-maxwell-underage-young ladies sex-jeffrey-epstein

Bilyeau, N. (2018, November 29). *What truly befell Natalie Wood? Town & Country; Town & Country*. https://www.townandcountrymag.com/society/tradition/a25242203/nat wood-passing/

Brewster, J. (2020, August 7). *'The Storm Is Here': GOP house competitor tweets QAnon rallying cry after Trump retweets her.* Forbes. https://www.forbes.com/locales/jackbrewster/2020/08/07/the-storm-is-here-gop-house-competitor tweets-qanon-mobilizing cry-after-trump-retweets-her/

Brown, D. L. (2017, October 26). The day John F. Kennedy was killed: How America mourned a fallen president. *The Washington Post*. https://www.washingtonpost.com/news/retropolis/wp/2017/10/26/how america-grieved john-f-kennedy-pictures of-despondency for-a-fallen-president/

Caffier, J. (2018, June 12). *A manual for QAnon, the new ruler of conservative conspiracy theories.* Www.Vice.Com. https://www.vice.com/en_us/article/ywex8v/what-is-qanon-trick theory

Calfas, J. (2017, October 5). *President Trump cautions of "the Calm Before the Storm" during military meeting.* Time. https://time.com/4971738/donald-trump-quiet/

Casaus, S. (2020, July 31). *Ghislaine Maxwell news: Horrifying subtleties from the unsealed documents.* Film Daily. https://filmdaily.co/news/ghislaine-maxwell-unlocked records/

Cassin, E., and Wendling, M. (2018, August 2). QAnon: What's reality behind a favorable to Trump fear inspired notion? BBC News. https://www.bbc.com/news/websites moving 45040614

Cherry, K. (2019, June 17). *Why individuals trust in paranoid fears.* Verywell Mind; Verywell Mind. https://www.verywellmind.com/why-individuals trust in-paranoid fears 4690335

Crawford, A. (2020, July 10). *A New World Order for the Coronavirus period is Coming.* Www.Bloomberg.Com. https://www.bloomberg.com/news/articles/2020-07-10/a-new-world-request for-the-Covid time is-emerging

Davies, D. (2020, August 20). *Columnist enters the universe of QAnon: "It's almost like a bad spy novel."* *NPR*.Org. https://www.npr.org/2020/08/20/904237192/columnist enters-the-universe of-qanon-it-is-nearly like-a-terrible covert operative novel

Diebel, M. (2018, October 10). *Anthony Weiner, ex-representative imprisoned for sexting with 15-year-old young lady, to be delivered ahead of schedule from jail.* USA TODAY. https://www.usatoday.com/story/news/country/2018/10/10/anthony-weiner-imprisoned sexting-young lady 15-gets-early-discharge/1587360002/

Dimuro, G. (2019, March 23). *The terrible full story behind the demise of Marilyn Monroe.* All That's Interesting; All That's Interesting.

https://allthatsinteresting.com/marilyn-monroe-death

Drabold, W. (2016, August 11). *Trump Will Keep Calling Clinton the Founder of ISIS*. Time. https://time.com/4448441/donald-trump-ISIS-author/

Editors, H. com. (2020, July 14). *JFK Jr. killed in plane accident.* HISTORY. https://www.history.com/this-day-ever/jfk-jr-killed-in-plane-crash

Evstatieva, M. (2020, July 10). *Life systems of a COVID-19 paranoid fear.* NPR.Org. https://www.npr.org/2020/07/10/889037310/life systems of-a-Coronavirus trick theory

Finstad, S. (2020, March 11). *"Natalie Wood's Drowning was not an accident": A new book's shocking findings.* Vanity Fair. https://www.vanityfair.com/hollywood/2020/03/natalie-wood-passing homicide robert-wagner-book

Fox, E. J. (2019, July 9). *"He said not to tell anybody": How Trump kept tabs on Jeffrey Epstein.* Vanity Fair. https://www.vanityfair.com/news/2019/07/how-trump-monitored jeffrey-epstein

Francescani, C. (2020, September 24). QAnon's development reflects sharp spike

in far-right extremist violence in US: Experts. *ABC.* https://abcnews.go.com/Politics/qanons-development mirrors-sharp-spike-fanatic savagery us/story?id=73079916

FriedenBerg, B. (2020). *The dull virality of a Hollywood blood-reaping connivance: A centuries-old enemy of Semitic fantasy is spreading unreservedly on extreme right corners of web-based media- - proposing another Computerized Dark Age has shown up.* Wored.Com. https://www.wored.com/story/assessment the-dim virality-or-a-hollywood-blood-reaping scheme/

Goertzel, T. (1994). Confidence in fear inspired notions. *Political Psychology, 15(4), 731*. https://doi.org/10.2307/3791630

Goldfield, D. (2019). *Deception and fear inspired notions regarding the Lincoln assassination.* Fords Theatre. https://www.fords.org/blog/post/deception and-paranoid notions about-the-lincoln-death/

Goodman, J., and Carmichael, F. (2020, May 30). The Bill Gates 'CPU' guarantee truth checked. *BBC News*. https://www.bbc.com/news/52847648

Gopnik, A. (2015, September 12). *Trump and Obama: A memorable night*. The New Yorker. https://www.newyorker.com/news/day by day remark/trump-and-obama-a memorable night/amp

Griffin, A. (2019, March 29). *There is an unusual fear inspired notion called QAnon. Here's what it actually is*. The Independent. https://www.independent.co.uk/way of life/devices and-tech/news/qanon-clarified what-trump-russia-examination pizzagate-a8845226.html

Grigoriadis, V. (2018, May 30). Inside Nxivm, the 'sex clique' that lectured empowerment. *The New York Times*. https://www.nytimes.com/2018/05/30/magazine/sex-clique strengthening nxivm-keith-raniere.html

Harrington, J., and Wood, M. (2020, January 12). *37 Famous Assassinations in American History - every minute of every day Wall St.* every minute of every day Wall St. https://247wallst.com/unique report/2018/04/25/37-popular deaths in-american-history/

Harrington, R. (2016, November 11). Here's what Trump means when he says, "Drain the swamp" - even though it's not an accurate metaphor. *Insider*.

Hernandez, I. (2016, November). *Meet the man who started the Illuminati*. Nationalgeographic.Com. https://www.nationalgeographic.com/history/magazine/2016/07-08/profile-adam-weishaupt-illuminati-secret-society/

HISTORY.com Editors. (2018, August 21). *Abraham Lincoln's Assassination*. HISTORY. https://www.history.com/topics/american-civil- war/abraham-lincoln-assassination

Hoke, Z. (2020, May 18). *Trump rejects Obama's criticism of his pandemic response | Voice of America - English*. Www.Voanews.Com. https://www.voanews.com/usa/trump-rejects-obamas-criticism-his-pandemic-response

Illing, S. (2020, May 13). *The "deep state" is real. But it's not what Trump thinks it is.* Vox. https://www.vox.com/policy-and-politics/2020/5/13/21219164/trump-deep-state-fbi-cia-david-rohde

Jenkins, N. (2015, July 27). *Hundreds gather for unveiling of Satanic statue in Detroit.* Time. https://time.com/3972713/detroit-satanic-statue-baphomet

Jessica Pearce Rotondi. (2019, December 11). *Five secret societies that have remained shrouded in mystery.* HISTORY. https://www.history.com/news/secret-societies-freemasons-knights-templar

Jung, E. A. (2017, November 2). *Man describes alleged sexual relationship with Kevin Spacey at 14.* Vulture. https://www.vulture.com/2017/11/kevin-spacey-alleged-sexual-relationship.html

Kelly, P. A. (2020, August 13). *Is the QAnon Jeffrey Epstein flight log fake? Everything to know.* Film Daily. https://filmdaily.co/news/qanon-flight-log/

Kim, S., and Perlin, P. (2019, March 25). *Recently unveiled NSA records shed further light on Five Eyes alliance.* Lawfare. https://www.lawfareblog.com/recently unveiled nsa-records shed-further-light-five-eyes-alliance

Kornhaber, S. (2018, December 27). *The upsetting truth regarding Kevin Spacey's 'Let me be frank' video.* The Atlantic. https://www.theatlantic.com/amusement/file/2018/12/kevin-spacey-let-me-be-forthcoming video-meaning/579034/

Kranc, L. (2020, August 23). *How NXIVM lured Hollywood stars and America's generally strong first class into an uncouth "sex clique." Esquire.* https://www.esquire.com/amusement/television/a33658764/what-is-nxivm-sex-faction famous people stars-the-pledges hbo-genuine story/

Lavender, J. (2020, August 6). *Marilyn Monroe kicked the bucket 'grasping chilling White House note from final phone call.'*

Mirror. https://www.mirror.co.uk/3am/big name news/marilyn-monroe-passed on gripping chilling-22478091

Levine, M. (2016, September 27). *Why Hillary Clinton erased 33,000 emails.* ABC News; ABC News. https://abcnews.go.com/Politics/hillary-clinton-erased 33000-messages secretary-state/story?id=42389308

Levitz, E. (2020, September 23). *QAnon is franticness. Be that as it may, having confidence in it can be rational.* Intelligencer. https://nymag.com/intelligencer/2020/09/why-qanon-pandemic-well known trump.html

Li, D. K. (2020, September 30). *NXIVM sex faction promoter Clare Bronfman condemned to over 6 years in jail.* NBC News. http://www.nbcnews.com/news/amp/ncna1241556

Louise, B. (2020, April 22). *Death in Hollywood: Was Marilyn Monroe murdered?* Film Daily. https://filmdaily.co/news/marilyn-monroe-scheme/

maskalunas.1. (2019, April 7). *The Illuminati vs. World Order | The psychology of extraordinary beliefs.* U.Osu.Edu. https://u.osu.edu/vanzandt/2019/04/07/the-illuminati-vs-world-order/comment-page-1/

Matthews, D. (2019, August 10). *The paranoid fears regarding the Clintons and Jeffrey Epstein's death, explained.* Vox. https://www.vox.com/2019/8/10/20800195/clintonbodycount-fear inspired notion jeffrey-epstein

Merriam-webster. (n.d.). Conspiracy theory. In Merriam-Webster. https://www.merriam-webster.com/word reference/conspiracy%20theory

Morgan, J. (2015, August 1). Interpreting the images on Satan's sculpture. *BBC News*. https://www.bbc.com/news/magazine-33682878

MorriS, B. S. (2013). *The total bonehead's manual for Freemasonry: Discover the rich and interesting history of this puzzling society (second ed.*, p. 65). Penguin.

Moynihan, C. (2020, August 28). Nxivm 'sex clique' pioneer ought to get life in prison, prosecutors say. *The New York Times*. https://www.nytimes.com/2020/08/28/nyregion/nxivm-keith-raniere-sentence.html

National Archives, and The Warren Commission. (2018, October 29). *Warren commission report*. National Archives. https://www.archives.gov/research/jfk/warren-commission-report

Nicholson, A. (2019, August 30). *Doubt creeps into the Five Eyes*. The Interpreter. https://www.lowyinstitute.org/the-mediator/doubt creeps-five-eyes

Nicolaou, E. (2019, November 25). *The subtleties of Princess Diana's awful 1997 death*. Oprah Magazine; Oprah Magazine. https://www.oprahmag.com/amusement/television motion pictures/a29874597/princess-diana-passing/

Ohlheiser, A. (2014, April 24). *A not-really short rundown of the relative multitude of things President Obama has bowed to*. The Atlantic. https://www.theatlantic.com/governmental issues/document/2014/04/a-not-really concise rundown of-the relative multitude of things-president-obama-has-bowed-to/361160/

OlmSted, K. S. (2019). *Genuine enemies : paranoid fears and American majority rule government, World War I to 9/11*. Oxford University Press.

Orden, E., and Hong, N. (2017, January 17). *Investigators weigh kid porn charges against Anthony Weiner*. Money Street Journal. https://www.wsj.com/articles/prosecuters-weigh-kid erotic entertainment charges-against-anthony-weiner-1485894771

Perez, M. (2020, August 19). *Trump will not upbraid QAnon after paranoid notion is portrayed to him*. Forbes. https://www.forbes.com/destinations/mattperez/2020/08/19/trump-will not censure qanon-after-paranoid notion is-portrayed to-him/

Pesca, M. (2020, September 15). *Everything that ISIS can say to us regarding QAnon*. Slate Magazine. https://slate.com/news-and-governmental issues/2020/09/qanon-clint-watts-isis-correlations substance transcript.html

Plumer, B. (2015, November 6). *The Keystone XL pipeline is dead. Here's why Obama killed it.* Vox. https://www.vox.com/2015/11/6/9681340/obama-rejects-cornerstone pipeline

Press, A. (2020, September 30). *Promoter of shamed Nxivm bunch pioneer sentenced to seven years in prison.* The Guardian. https://www.theguardian.com/us-news/2020/sep/30/nxivm-bunch pioneer promoter jail sentence

Relman, E. (2017, November 16). *These are the rape charges against Bill Clinton.* The Independent. https://www.independent.co.uk/news/world/america/bill-clinton-rape charges embarrassment monica-lewinsky-a8058576.html

RIchardson, I. (2020, June 29). *Reality check: Posts call for evacuation of sinister statues in cities where there aren't any.* USA TODAY. https://www.usatoday.com/story/news/factcheck/2020/06/29/reality check-sinister sculptures arent-found arkansas-detroit/3264174001

Roberts, K. (2020, May 9). *Natalie Wood's girl and spouse stand up about her death in new doc.* Harper's BAZAAR. https://www.harpersbazaar.com/culture/film-television/a32420871/natalie-wood-passing evident story-course of events/

Rodriguez, S., and Caputo, M. (2020, September 14). *'This is f- - - ing insane': Florida Latinos overwhelmed by wild paranoid ideas.* POLITICO. https://www.politico.com/news/2020/09/14/florida-latinos-disinformation-413923

Rogers, T. N. (2019, August 11). *The renowned associations of Jeffrey Epstein, the tip top abundance director who passed on while in prison while anticipating preliminary on sex trafficking charges.* Business Insider US. https://www.businessinsider.co.za/moving/celebrities jeffrey-epstein-cash supervisor sexual-dealing associated 2019-7

Ross, K. (2020, August 25). *What is QAnon and for what reason is it drawing in so many followers in Australia?*

SouthChina Morning Post. https://www.scmp.com/week-asia/legislative issues/article/3098690/what-qanon-and-why-it-drawing in so-many-supporters australia

Rothbard, M. (2006). Radio free Rothbard. *Diary of Libertarian Studies, 20(2), 17-51*. As cited by R. M. Marcus.

Rupp, K. (2016, December 24). *Obama's drapery call: A think back on a legacy of executive overreach.* TheHill. https://thehill.com/sites/savants blog/the-organization/311608-obamas-shade get back to a-look on-a-heritage of

Sanburn, J. (2016, June 9). *The world's most powerful and secret group, explained.* Time. https://time.com/4362872/bilderberg-bunch gatherings 2016-paranoid ideas/

Sebastian, M. (2016, December 5). *Indeed, even the Pizzagate speculate no longer believes the conspiracy theory.* Esquire. https://www.esquire.com/news-legislative issues/news/a51268/what-is-pizzagate/

Shalby, C. (2018). *The death of Robert Kennedy, as told 50 years later*. Latimes.Com. https://www.latimes.com/projects/la-na-robert-f-kennedy/

Shapiro, I. (2017, January 19). *Top 10 different ways Obama disregarded the constitution during his Presidency.* Cato Institute. https://www.cato.org/distributions/critique/top-10-ways-obama-abused constitution-during-presidency

Silverstein, K. (2015, March 25). *The Jeffrey Epstein issue jeopardizes Hillary Clinton's Presidential prospects.* Observer. https://observer.com/2015/03/the-jeffrey-epstein-issue jeopardizes hillary-clintons-official possibilities/

Smith, D. (2016, November 1). The Hillary Clinton email discussion explained: what we know so far. *The Guardian.* https://www.theguardian.com/us-news/2016/oct/31/hillary-clinton-most recent messages explained

Smith, S. (2013, November 22). *Accused JFK assassin is arrested, then gunned down*. Cbsnews.Com. https://www.cbsnews.com/news/jfk-death suspect-lee-harvey-oswald-is-captured then-gunned-down/

Spring, M., and Wendling, M. (2020, September 3). What links coronavirus myths and QAnon? *BBC News*. https://www.bbc.com/news/sites moving 53997203

Stanford, C. (2020, March 11). Covid, Joe Biden, Harvey Weinstein: Your Wednesday instructions. *The New York Times*. https://www.nytimes.com/2020/03/11/instructions/Covid joe-biden-harvey-weinstein.html

Stracqualursi, V. (2020, September 24). *New York Times: Prosecutor tapped by Barr to investigate Russia probe is now looking into Clinton Foundation*. CNN. https://www.cnn.com/2020/09/24/legislative issues/durham-examination clinton-establishment/index.html

Stuewe, V. (2020, September 4). *The creepiest photographs of the Jeffrey Epstein island: You need to see these*. Film Daily.

https://filmdaily.co/news/jeffrey-epstein-island-frightening photographs/

T.C. Sottek. (2013, July 17). *All that you really want to be familiar with PRISM*. The Verge; The Verge. https://www.theverge.com/2013/7/17/4517480/nsa-spying-crystal observation cheat-sheet

Transmit Reporters. (2017, August 29). *Princess Diana: What occurred the evening of her passing? The Telegraph.* https://www.telegraph.co.uk/imperial family/0/princess-diana-happened-night-passing/

Tenbarge, K. (2020, March 18). *A QAnon paranoid idea about Oprah Winfrey went so popular that it incited her to answer, showing the scope of coronavirus misinformation*. Insider. https://www.insider.com/qanon-oprah-winfrey-illegal exploitation capture paranoid fear twitter-Covid 2020-3

The Great Seal of the United States. (n.d.). *The Great Seal of the United States - America's vision explanation*. Www.Greatseal.Com. https://www.greatseal.com

Trotter, J. K. (2019, July 12). *Flight information from Jeffrey Epstein's personal luxury planes show an extravagant itinerary as the dividers shut in*. Insider. https://www.insider.com/jeffrey-epsteins-personal luxury plane flight-information 2019-7

Varshavski, M. (2020, May 14). *Point-by-Point "Plandemic" smackdown*. Www.Youtube.Com. https://www.medpagetoday.com/infectiousdisease/covid19/86487

Voytko, L. (2019, August 9). *Unlocked Jeffrey Epstein archives list new allegations against powerful men*. Forbes. https://www.forbes.com/locales/lisettevoytko/2019/08/09/unlocked jeffrey-epstein-archives list-new-charges against-influential men/

Walker, J. (2014). *The United States of paranoia : a connivance theory*. Harper Perennial.

Wessel, H. (1996, February 7). *Resigned instructor reviews reality "White Squall."* *Orlandosentinel*.Com. https://www.orlandosentinel.com/news/os-xpm-1997-02-07-9602061059-story.html

Zoellner, D. (2020, September 4). *Joe Biden says QAnon allies should get a mental health check*. The Independent. https://www.independent.co.uk/news/world/americas/us-political race/joe-biden-qanon-emotional wellness trump-fear inspired notion a9706286.html

Printed in Great Britain
by Amazon

17690910R00059